RIO DE JANEIRO

By Douglas Botting
and the Editors of Time-Life Books

With Photographs by Art Kane

THE GREAT CITIES · TIME-LIFE BOOKS · AMSTERDAM

The Author: Douglas Botting was born in London in 1934. His first book, about his travels in Arabia, was published while he was still an undergraduate at Oxford. He subsequently worked as a photographer and television film-maker in many parts of the world and wrote several books of travel and biography, including *One Chilly Siberian Morning, Humboldt and the Cosmos* and, for TIME-LIFE Books, *Wilderness Europe*. A frequent visitor to Rio, he has made a number of expeditions to unexplored regions of the Brazilian interior.

The Photographer: Born in 1925, Art Kane is a graduate of the Cooper Union School of Art in New York City. Before he became a photographer, he spent 11 years working as an editorial art director for various magazines. In both fields he has won numerous awards for excellence, and many of his pictures are in permanent collections, including the Museum of Modern Art and the Metropolitan Museum of Art in New York.

EDITOR: George Constable
Design Consultant: Louis Klein
Chief Designer: Graham Davis
Director of Photography: Pamela Marke

Editorial Staff for Rio
Deputy Editor: Simon Rigge
Designer: Eric Molden
Staff Writers: Tony Allan, Mike Brown,
Norman Kolpas, Alan Lothian
Picture Editor: Karin Pearce
Text Researcher: Sue Dawson
Design Assistants: Martin Gregory, Fiona Preston

Editorial Production for the Series
Art Department: Julia West
Editorial Department: Ellen Brush, Molly Sutherland
Picture Department: Thelma Gilbert, Brigitte Guimpier

The captions and the texts accompanying the photographs in this volume were prepared by the editors of TIME-LIFE Books.

Valuable assistance was given in the preparation of this volume by Barry Hillenbrand, Rio correspondent for TIME magazine.

Published by TIME-LIFE International (Nederland) B.V.
Otto Heldringstraat 5, Amsterdam 1018.

ISBN 7054 0490 0

Cover: Traffic on Rio's six-lane Avenida Atlântica pours past the gleaming, 100-yard-wide expanse of Copacabana beach, whose name is almost a synonym for tropical pleasure.

First end paper: The mosaic pattern of Copacabana's promenade seems to echo the waves that are just steps away. Throughout Rio, mosaic pavements line wide avenues and enliven the main squares.

Last end paper: Soccer players line up for a free-kick during a match held in Rio's Maracanã Stadium. Their club, América, is one of the most popular in this soccer-mad metropolis.

Contents

I

The Siren Song of Rio

I was always dreaming of sailing down to Rio when I was a boy. Often I prepared to sail to the Americas by tea-time, casting off the hawsers that tied me to the here and now in England, and tuning my ears like sea shells to hear the roaring of the breakers on the reefs of faraway shores. I made many such imaginary voyages—in barques and brigantines, schooners and men-o'-war, in the Roaring Forties, Sargasso Sea and Straits of Zanzibar—but my voyage to Rio was always intended to be the most illustrious of them all. I knew little about the place, and even into adult life I continued to believe that it was situated at the mouth of the Amazon, the only other name I immediately associated with Brazil. But the connotations and reverberations of the very words, Rio de Janeiro, remained boundlessly exotic and exciting. And they still do.

In this, I think I am not alone. Rio is one of those favoured places of the earth whose names maintain a universal romantic appeal. Like Tahiti or Bali, it seems to offer the possibility of a different kind of life. Rio is not a great historical city like Florence or Venice. It is not a spiritual city like Jerusalem. It is not an intellectual city like Paris, or a great commercial city like New York, or a political city like Berlin, or even a capital city like London. It is a sensual city. Its song is a siren song, its votaries are lotus-eaters, its promise is the promise of a Never Never Land, its denizens are Peter Pans who have attained puberty.

Many years were to pass before I set eyes on Rio de Janeiro, and my journey, when it finally began, was attended by elements of comedy. I was making preparations for a long, photographic expedition through the Amazon region of Brazil, and since this was to be my first visit to the New World I felt it would be appropriate to arrive there in the time-honoured way, by sea rather than by air. It was not easy to find a ship at short notice, but eventually I was offered a berth on a Swedish cargo vessel that was on the point of sailing from Gothenburg for the east coast ports of South America. If I liked, the shipping company informed me, I could have the owner's suite, which had remained unbooked, for the price of an ordinary cabin. It was thus in some style that I prepared at last to sail down to Rio.

The old grey ship lay at the Gothenburg quayside as still and seemingly abandoned as the Flying Dutchman. But when I began to unload my baggage from the taxi, I became aware of a figure rattling down the gangway towards me. He was a chubby man dressed in ordinary casual clothes.

"You coming on board?" he asked in a Swedish accent when he got to the bottom of the gangway.

In the heart of Rio, the early 20th-Century Municipal Theatre—a two-thirds replica of the Paris Opéra—is dwarfed by office towers. With a growth rate twice that of Brazil as a whole, the city has sacrificed most of its architectural past to high-rise construction.

"Yes," I announced, drawing myself up to my full height. "I have reserved the owner's suite."

The man eyed me up and down and cast a glance over my travel-worn impedimenta. "The owner's suite?" he asked. "Let me take your bags."

What an obliging salt, I thought. What a jolly tar. I loaded him up with my cases. I hung them round his neck, balanced them on his shoulders, tucked them under his arm, until he lurched and swayed under the weight.

"That all?" he said, perspiration breaking out on his brow. "Let's go."

Thus unburdened, I lightly stepped off the Old World and embarked on the first stage of my journey to the New. I followed the man up the gangway, into the ship, along passages and through bulkhead doors, until at last we came to a spacious and amply appointed suite of cabins overlooking the bow. As the man discharged his cargo, I rummaged in my pocket for a coin to reward him for his services. But he forestalled me. He extended his right hand towards me and, before I could drop the coin into it, he grasped my own hand and exclaimed: "May I introduce myself? I am your captain. We sail within the hour. Would you like some gin?"

And so we sailed down to Rio.

At 12 knots the grey ship stoutly breasted the green ocean swell and brought us every day to more and more southerly latitudes.

After the Bay of Biscay we began to plough the 5,000-mile route of the Portuguese navigators, colonizers, immigrants, and slaves who laid the foundations of Brazil. Past Madeira, the Canaries, the Mauritanian coast of Africa and the Cape Verde Islands, we followed in the wake of Captain André Gonçalves, who discovered the site of Rio in 1502, and Estácio de Sá, who founded the city in 1565, and the Prince Regent of Portugal, Dom João, who settled there with his royal court in 1808. We crossed the Tropic of Cancer, and the sun burned down on us and the deck grew hot. The flying fish flew, the whales sounded, the Portuguese men-of-war floated past on the slow ocean current. Our lives settled into a steady rhythm that was governed by the rising of the sun to starboard and its setting to larboard. The captain proffered gin, threw parties, played the gramophone and dallied with the lonely Swedish wives who constituted most of the small complement of passengers. In all that great circle of water we never saw another funnel or mast.

By the time we crossed the Equator we were nearer the New World than the Old, and a beguiling tropical languor settled over the ship—a compound of heat, confinement and ennui. It was as though some emanation from the land, some distillation of the spirit of the place had wafted out to us, beyond the farthest limits of the skuas and drifting coconuts and silt washed out to sea from the mouths of the rivers. The nights were invariably beautiful, the Southern Cross clearly visible, the moonlight on the water as straight and bright as an airport flarepath.

Two Cariocas—as the people of Rio are called—dally for a moment in a café off Ipanema Beach, a favourite haunt of rich and trendy holidaymakers in summer.

Then one day we picked up Rio radio on the wireless in the captain's cabin. It was very faint, for we were on the very edge of its range, but next day it was stronger, and we sat for a long time listening to the sounds from across the sea. I had been taking my first faltering steps in Brazilian Portuguese under the guidance of a young woman on board. Alas, when I heard the language on the radio I did not understand a word of it. I could only listen to the sounds, the rhythm, the aural ambience. Brazilian seemed a sensuous, sweet, plangent language, all vowels and music, drawl and twang. It was language of the tropics, of verandah and swaying palm, of swinging hammock and brownskin girl.

Very often the radio played a song of Rio—*Garôta de Ipanema*, "Girl from Ipanema"—with a melody so seductive that it became the hit of the ship; its syncopation seemed to fit the throbbing of the ship's engines, its mood seemed to suit my own: "Olha que coisa mais linda, Mais cheia de graça. . . . Tall and tan and young and lovely, the Girl from Ipanema goes walking. And when she passes, each one she passes goes 'a-a-h!' . . . "

These were the first vibrations I picked up from the New World, the first intimations I received from that city of hope and illusion, Rio de Janeiro.

We had been at sea for more than three weeks and were drawing near to the Tropic of Capricorn before we caught sight of land. Early one morning I felt a freezing wind off the sea—a novelty after so many sweltering days —and saw a high green headland to starboard. This was Cabo Frio, or Cape Cold, the first landmark on the approaches to Rio. For days we had been sailing on a southerly bearing, parallel with the coast of Brazil, which for thousands of miles runs approximately north-south. Now we turned to follow an indentation in the coast that starts at Cabo Frio and stretches east-west. Rio lies in the middle of this indentation, facing not east towards Africa, as many people imagine, but south towards Antarctica.

All morning we sailed along that coastline, and schools of dolphins, which relished the cold currents off the Cape, sped out to join us and leapt high out of the water from beneath our bows. We had barely sat down to lunch when the captain summoned us to the bridge. We were approaching Rio, he said. We could eat later.

It is not easy to recapture the state of excitement in which I watched the scattered elements of the view—mountains and forests, ocean and beaches—resolve themselves into a coherent picture of Rio from the sea. It was a day of dramatic skies. Blue-black cumulus clouds rolled round the summits of the mountains, drawing shadows across the tropical greenery that covered the hills. The sun shone between the clouds in celestial beams that radiated outwards like the spokes of a wheel. Humpbacked islands lay scattered about like a school of resting whales. On top of a tall peak, clearly visible from far out at sea, an immense statue of Christ with outstretched hands disappeared and reappeared among the clouds like a Boeing jetliner. Some 2,000 feet or more below the statue, squeezed between mountains and the sea like plaster of Paris in a mould, lay the city: an unbroken line of brilliant white skyscrapers whose rectangular façades gleamed in the sun. From such a distance, the city presented a curiously ethereal aspect. No noise emanated from it, no smells, no squalor, no signs of its human inhabitants. Poised insubstantially between air and water, Rio seemed a dream city—the most beautiful place in the world.

As we came in closer, I looked out from the bridge, identifying places from the chart. We were approaching the narrow opening of Guanabara Bay, a huge, balloon-shaped natural harbour on whose western shore the centre of the city lies. So large and impressive is Guanabara Bay that when Captain Gonçalves entered it on January 1, 1502, he thought he had found a great river, and from this mistake the city got its name: Rio de Janeiro, the River of January.

As we drew level with the bay we were no more than a quarter of a mile from the land, and the city's humped and angular mountain profile rose before us against the tropical sky. The immense bulk of Rio's silhouette has been called the Sleeping Giant; seen from a certain direction, it resembles a human form stretched out on its back. The giant's head lies in the Tijuca mountains behind the city, with the peak of Tijuca as his nose. His high flank extends above the length of Rio, and his upturned feet are represented by Sugar Loaf mountain, named after the conical loaves of refined sugar once produced on the Portuguese island of Madeira.

Sugar Loaf stands on the west side of the entrance to the bay. Behind it towers the peak of Corcovado, surmounted by the statue of Christ, and along the coast to the west is Copacabana, that ellipse of brilliant white sand that the people of Rio consider a beach without equal. We steamed slowly past the beach and trained our field-glasses on the little brown figures that inhabited it. After a rocky headland, we came to the second ellipse of Ipanema and Leblon beaches, with a crust of umbrellas like coloured buttons and the ocean coming to an end in a long line of foaming surf.

"Olha que coisa . . . " went the ship's loudspeakers. "When she walks she's like a samba that swings so cool and sways so gentle, that when she passes, each one she passes goes 'a-a-h!' . . . "

I stared entranced as the land slid by, mouthing the names bequeathed to the mountains and headlands and bays long ago by Tupi-speaking Indian tribes: Tijuca, Jacarepaguá, Itapeba, Sernambetiba, Itapuca, Guaratiba. Signs of habitation had petered out by now and the coast seemed as virgin as the day Gonçalves first clapped eyes on it.

"So," said the captain, glad to have put on a good show. "That was Rio."

"Wonderful!" I replied. And then I asked: "When do we land?"

"Land?" said the captain. "We don't land. We have no cargo in Rio. Our next stop is Santos. Would you like some gin?"

So my voyage to Rio, the realization of a dream of half a lifetime, did not end quite as I had expected. The ship's agents in Rio had advised the

Standing bold against the darkening coastal mountains, Sugar Loaf peak guards the entrance to the immense natural harbour of Guanabara Bay and the smaller, yacht-flecked inlet of Botafogo Bay (foreground). Central Rio lies on the western shore of Guanabara Bay.

captain over the radio telephone that there was no cargo to pick up there, and so we steamed straight past. Instead of sailing through the seaward portals of the city in my owner's suite, I arrived a week later through the back streets in a clanking bus. I stayed in Rio for some weeks before departing for the interior of Brazil. In the years that followed I was to return four more times, and during those visits I learned at last to recognize which part of the dream was reality and which part of the reality was dream.

The first day of my latest visit to Rio was a day of mixed fortunes and strange impressions. Returning to the city from a wintery Europe after a long absence, I was subjected to a violent sensory assault, a kind of mortar attack of exotic images and sounds that left me dazed. At tea-time on the previous day I had been in London, where a hard northerly wind sniped along darkened alleys and the crowds swept by with wan winter faces, like dead souls. Now it was breakfast time in a tropical city, and although the sun had not been up an hour, the morning was already hot.

In the back of the taxi that brought me to my hotel overlooking the beach of Copacabana, my body sweated profusely while my mind turned numb. It was the morning rush-hour. The streets were jammed with pedestrians, buses and commuter cars. My driver drove at a suicidal pace. He dodged and swerved around other cars and seemed to aim his taxi at pedestrians. So did everyone else. This was normal, I remembered. Rio has one of the worst traffic accident records in the world, and more than 2,000 people a year are killed in the streets, or one every three hours. Every day you see a car upside down on the beach, or a bus that has crashed into a shop window, or a crowd chasing some driver who is running away from the scene of an accident. The squeal of tyres, the clunk of metal and the wailing of sirens is the leit-motif of the Rio streets.

By the time I had been in Rio half an hour, I was suitably prepared for any eventuality. It was therefore with clinical detachment that, stopped by some traffic lights at a T-junction next to a cemetery, I watched as a stoutish, middle-aged woman crossing the road in front of me was cut down by a motor-cyclist. As if in slow-motion replay, I saw the motor-cyclist brake and begin to skid. His right handle-bar scythed the woman down at 40 miles an hour, and the man flew off his bike and rode through space, still in the correct motor-cycling position, then slid along the tarmac on his elbows into the path of an approaching Jeep, which swerved with a squeal of tyres and mounted the pavement, sending passers-by running for safety. The woman by now had been hauled to her feet by two helpers, but her head lolled and her feet bent at strange angles.

The traffic lights turned green and the taxi-driver spun the wheel left and drove at high speed from the scene of the accident. Two hundred yards down the road, he stopped next to a policeman on traffic duty.

"There's been a woman knocked down up the road," he said and sped

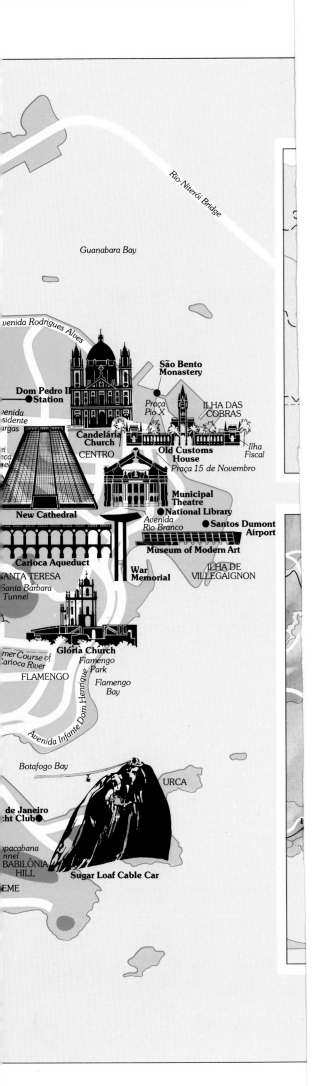

off before the policeman could take his number. He didn't want to be a witness, he wanted nothing to do with the police at all. No one in Rio does.

We came to Copacabana and burst into the space and light of the wide seafront thoroughfare, the Avenida Atlântica, with its pavement mosaics and bright seafront bars and terraced restaurants.

"Do you think she was killed?" I asked the driver when we got to my hotel. The taxi-driver nodded. "Dead," he said in a matter-of-fact tone. "That will be a hundred cruzeiros. Haven't you got anything smaller?"

By now my dream of Rio as a city of lotus-eaters and infinite romantic promise was shattered. Reality took over. Rio I knew then, if I had not known it before, was a mortal city like any other, inhabited by people preoccupied with the daily realities of the human condition, with living and dying, getting and spending in a world where fate was blind.

Those daily realities in Rio are complicated by some especially trying problems. Rio is one of the fastest growing cities in Brazil; but because mountains occupy so much of its land area, the extra inhabitants must either go and live on the distant outskirts or else become more and more crowded within the existing urban areas. Add to this geographical problem a disorganized bureaucracy, inadequate sanitation and transport systems, unemployment as high as 15 per cent and a rate of inflation varying between 20 and 80 per cent—and you have something close to chaos.

Until 1960 Rio was the capital of Brazil, but in that year it handed over this role to the new city of Brasília in the distant interior, and it is now simply capital of its own state of Rio de Janeiro. It used to be the commercial centre of Brazil, too, but that role has been usurped by São Paulo, Brazil's great boom city. So what is the function of the city now?

If Rio is no longer the leading city of Brazil, it is nevertheless still the only city which is an administrative, cultural, university, industrial, shipping, commercial and banking centre and at the same time a beach resort open all the year round—Brazil's biggest holiday attraction. Now more than ever, Rio stands for fun, expressed most notably through the popular outlets of Carnival, football and the beach. The Carnival festivities before Lent are far more riotous in Rio than in other cities with similar celebrations. The great football clubs of Rio play the game with more uninhibited talent and with far noisier crowds than most teams anywhere. As for the beach, it is to Rio what cuisine is to Paris: the essence of its soul.

To the inhabitants of one of the most densely populated places in the world, the beach is the great escape. Without it they would become neurotic, as the citizens of São Paulo, which has no beach, are said to be. There are innumerable beaches in Rio, but on a fine morning at the height of the holiday season, they are all so packed that it seems as though the entire population has taken to the edge of the sea like an army awaiting evacuation—or, as one reporter from São Paulo put it, "like the crowds of the faithful on the banks of the Ganges". "Crabs" is what the French

Tijuca National Park

Tijuca Forest

ALTO DA BOA VISTA

CANOA

▲Gávea

ROC

Gávea Golf Club●

Lagoa-Barra Highway

SÃO CONRADO

Doi

Hotel Naçional

N

called the early Portuguese settlers in Rio in the 16th Century; and crabs they are still, scuttling about the sands and compulsively roasting in the sun.

By far the most popular beaches in Rio are Copacabana, Ipanema and Barra da Tijuca. Copacabana and Ipanema, together with the skyscrapers behind them, constitute what is known as the South Zone, a strip of land along the Atlantic so narrowly compressed between the mountains and the sea that it is only five streets deep at the western end and only three streets deep at its eastern end. Yet the South Zone contains fully one-sixth of the population of the city, and its skyscraper apartments are among the most coveted and expensive living units in the world. Here are found the smart, the swinging, the chic and the rich. An apartment in the South Zone is the up-country millionaire's ambition and retirement dream, the one place in Brazil he would choose. The South Zone is what people abroad or in the interior think of when they hear the name Rio. It is, in effect, a second city, whose only connections with the central and northern parts of the metropolis are three tunnels running through the hills.

I breakfasted my first morning, as I was to breakfast every morning, on the fruits of the country: the juice of the cashew or the maracujá, the flesh of the guava, pawpaw, melon or fruta-de-conde, and strong black Brazilian coffee. My table looked out on to Copacabana beach. It was February, the middle of the antipodean summer and the height of the Brazilian holiday season. An extraordinary vitality filled the city, a restless energy and exuberance. People drifted in an unending stream out of the deep shadows of the side streets into the blinding sunshine of the Avenida Atlântica: bikini-clad young girls tanned to the colour of chocolate; millionaires with borzoi dogs; bronzed youths with cut-off jeans; mothers in strapless beachrobes called *tomara-que-caia*, meaning "If only it would fall"; pot-bellied old men in shorts standing motionless in the first patches of sunlight they came to, their faces turned upwards to the sky, eyes shut, absorbing the warmth and radiation like lizards on a rock.

I changed and went down to the beach. There was no breeze off the sea this morning. Brilliant butterflies from the forested mountains above the city fluttered across the sands, and huge frigate birds with seven-foot wing-spans and long forked tails soared over the penthouse suites of the apartment blocks, circling effortlessly on the thermals above the softening asphalt. I struggled through the soft sand to the edge of the sea and set up my bivouac—beach mat and sunshade and towel—among the other encampments near the pounding surf.

The beach was as blinding as the Sahara. Even under my umbrella the heat reflected off the white sand was scorching, and to this day I carry two permanent sun-burn scars incurred in the first hour on that beach. Even the beach-lovers of Rio are deeply lacerated by the sun and suffer an abnormal incidence of skin cancer as a result of heavy doses of ultra-

Arms outstretched in a gesture of divine forgiveness, a 700-ton concrete figure of Christ the Redeemer reigns over downtown Rio from the 2,307-foot peak of Corcovado. At that height, the statue is often veiled by cloud or mountain mist and, when floodlit (right), appears to shed unearthly rays of glory.

violet rays; many of them paint their noses with a thick white zinc oxide paste to block out the sun, and go around looking like Carnival clowns.

It would be a mistake to think that the beach was a place of repose. It was, in fact, as full of bustle as the streets. Along the promenade at its inshore edge, men ran about in packs, doing their Coopers. (Cooper is the name of an American doctor who wrote a highly successful keep-fit book that involved running a certain distance in a certain time every day; the Avenida Atlântica is now marked off in measured lengths for the benefit of joggers, who call these lengths Coopers.) Close to the surf, elderly sun-worshippers did physical jerks by slowly waving their limbs about like chameleons, while younger bloods sweated and strained at pull-ups and press-ups on gymnastic apparatus erected at various points along the beach, or played football with unflagging vigour in the soft sand and burn-ing sun, emulating their heroes in the great Brazilian World Cup squad.

In the sea extraordinary-looking youths surfed on the big rollers, their sunburnt mahogany skins gleaming underwater like polished wood, their shoulder-length hair turned straw-blond by applications of paraffin wax used on surf boards. It was a very physical place, this beach—very pre-occupied with how one looked, with fitness, body sculpting, sun tan, and the hedonistic pleasures of sea and sand. Among the thickets of umbrella poles, girls were scattered about in scanty bikinis called *tangas*, which were extremely small and left little to the imagination. They were very lovely, some of these tropical Aphrodites. Exquisite of form and supple of limb, they lay on the burning sand in a kind of voluptuary trance, like the naked slave girls in the friezes decorating Tutankhamen's tomb.

The sense of touch was the predominant channel of communication here. People were constantly rubbing oil into their skin or someone else's, or pouring water over themselves out of little plastic buckets, or adjusting their *tangas*. Little carnal intimacies, of a frank but curiously innocent kind, reinforced a wide range of human relationships: a father fondled his teenage daughter's waist, casually, almost absent-mindedly rolling the little fold of flesh above her hip between his thumb and index and second finger, as if he were sampling the texture of silk; a young man fluttered around his girlfriend, a startling creature of almost pure Amerindian descent—who could she be, why should she be here, so far from the Amazon tributaries?—and stroked the tresses of her long, jet black hair.

While the gilded youth of Copacabana—and their not-so-gilded elders—indulged themselves in a ritual narcissism, the real athletes of the beach plied their trade. Hour after hour, in a temperature that registered nearly 100°F in the shade, beach vendors trudged relentlessly through the soft sand, each man carrying two large, 30-kilo metal drums of lemonade, cold tea, Coca-Cola or beer. "*Alô, alô,*" one cried, "*Dona Joana, tomando limonada você vai ficar bacana.*" (Hallo, hallo, Lady Joanna, if you drink lemonade you'll become beautiful.)

A smashed guard-rail along a curve is the epitaph for an over-enthusiastic motorist. This route through Rio's southern outskirts is only one of many hillside highways in the city— dangerous enough even without the open- throttle style of most Carioca drivers.

The beach vendors were virtually the only black people on Copacabana beach. This is not what you might expect in Brazil, where 20 per cent of the population is black, and nearly 30 per cent is of mixed blood and where, officially at least, there is no racial discrimination. And yet, in Rio, as elsewhere in Brazil, you quickly discover that people of different colours do not have the same status. Most of the men and women who do the dirty, heavy or menial jobs in the city are black. Although white people may pride themselves on the lack of a colour problem in Rio, the truth is that the darker your skin, the lower down the social scale and the more poverty-stricken you are. Perhaps that is not so surprising, considering that African slavery lasted longer in Brazil than in any other Western country; it was not abolished until 1888. The social attitudes and economic stratification that went with slavery have clearly persisted to the present day. I watched an elderly black man with grizzled hair stagger through the sand with a huge basket of pineapples on his head and the bare blade of a knife clenched between his teeth, and I thought: what a place this is to be rich in, what a place to be poor!

I decided to brave the surf. Swimming from Rio's open ocean-facing beaches can be a dangerous business. Hardly a week passes without a bathing fatality, and in the holiday season there can be as many as 10 a day. The papers that morning carried reports of two people drowned on the previous day and 17 rescued from drowning; and I met numerous people with limbs in plaster after accidents in the surf.

When I took the plunge I was caught off guard by the rapidity with which one big breaker can succeed another, and I was nearly smashed down on to the sandy bottom. But on my second attempt I swam out until I was in the gentle swell beyond the line of breakers. The sea was warm and lovely there, and strangely quiet after the commotion of the beach. Butterflies, lost and disoriented and looking for terra firma, fluttered southwards over the water in the direction of Antarctica. Shoals of small fish, pursued by unseen predators, attempted to leap out of the sea all around me; the water fizzed and flashed with their panic efforts to escape, and as the waves curled over I could see the fish clearly in the translucent breakers, preserved for an instant in jade green crystal. Out at sea a submarine from the navy base in Guanabara Bay overhauled a two-masted schooner beating down to Argentina. The skyscrapers of the Avenida Atlântica rose and fell with the motion of the sea, sinking and reappearing beyond the horizon of the waves like an ocean liner on a cruise. Behind the skyscrapers, Rio's huge statue of Christ peered down from its mountaintop, looming in permanent benediction over the city.

The vastness of the ocean horizon and the long sweeps of gleaming sand, I realized then, give Rio an illusion of infinite space. But in another sense, the seafront merely underlines the constraints of life in the city. It is a frontier beyond which the city cannot extend, one of two great natural

Prodigal sunshine and rain combine to provide Rio with an endless abundance of fresh produce. On the left, a street-market vendor presides over a mini-mountain of locally grown oranges; above, one of the stallholders tempts shoppers with an exotic array of condiments, including bags of peppers that he will grind on the spot.

barriers between which Rio is eternally trapped. The other barrier is the celebrated backdrop of Rio's mountains, which mark the beginning of Brazil's vast tropic interior and form the dominant feature of the so-called Sertão Carioca, the Rio backlands of forests, plains, marshes and lagoons.

The peaks and ridges and hills of Rio are offshoots of an ancient gneiss-granite mountain chain, the Serra do Mar, that stretches down the coast of Brazil for 1,500 miles between Bahia in the north and Pôrto Alegre in the south. They soar up all over the city, a delight to the eye and a penance to the road builders and town planners who must lay down the infrastructure of a growing metropolis among them. No city on earth can be so disorientating as Rio. Driving through the streets, your route twists and turns round hills and mountain spurs, dives through tunnels and winds through passes until you have as little sense of direction or where-abouts as a child on a fun-fair whirligig.

The massifs known as the Serra da Tijuca and the Serra da Carioca are the most immediate in the life of Rio, the most beautiful and the most tortured by folds and faults. Their best known scarps and spurs have names coined by the early Portuguese sailors: apart from Pão de Açúcar (Sugar Loaf) and Corcovado (Hunchback), there is Leme (Rudder), Arpoador (Harpooner), Dois Irmãos (Two Brothers) and Gávea (Topsail). They sweep down to the sea and nudge their way into the centre of the city, where their luxuriant plant life threatens to colonize the streets and invade suburban gardens. Together these massifs of Rio form an area of tropical wilderness roughly shaped like a triangle. The triangle tapers towards the entrance of Guanabara Bay and divides Rio into two unequal parts: the narrow South Zone along the Atlantic, and the city centre and North Zone lying in the plains along the shore of Guanabara Bay.

The best place from which to survey both parts of the city is on top of the granite peak of Corcovado, at the apex of the triangle, and the most adventurous way to get to Corcovado is the back way, through the rain forests of the Serra da Tijuca, a hundred square miles of wilderness which are now protected as a national park. Nowhere else can you better appreciate the prodigality of tropical nature in Rio. As soon as you leave the congested streets behind and begin to climb into the mountains, you enter a world of uncontrolled vegetable effervescence, where plants and creepers writhe around each other in an arboreal parody of erotic Hindu temple carvings. The trees are very high and straight, with great roots and tangled canopies, where woolly-faced monkeys shriek and jeer as you pass by; thick lianas hang down like pythons and branches are furry with green moss and sprouting orchids and other epiphytes of all kinds. There are huge tree ferns, bamboos, bougainvillaeas, passionflowers, flamboyants, magnificent trumpet trees and Brazilian spider flower trees; you can also find sago palms, lobsterclaws, jacarandas, jequitibas, begonias with yellow blossoms full of growling bees, and great wild fruit trees like the *jaca* or jackfruit tree, whose 30-pound fruits are the largest in the world.

Plenty of wild animals still live in the forests overlooking Rio. The caymen have been hunted out of the pools in the last half-century, and there are no longer any sloths or jaguars. But there are still parrots, possums, anteaters, armadillos, racoons, coatis, bush dogs and fatally venomous jararaca snakes, all within earshot of the steady purring of Volkswagens and Chevrolets in the thoroughfares of the city.

As I reached the top of Corcovado, the land fell away sharply on all sides, and black vultures soared and circled in the void on outstretched wings. At the base of the statue of Christ there is a viewing platform, and from here you look out over the most dazzling urban panorama in the world. Staring down, I could see almost the whole of the city and all its natural setting. Close to me, at the entrance to Guanabara Bay, rose the high hump of Sugar Loaf, with the fashionable enclave of Botafogo Bay to its left. To the right of it, outside the bay and round to the west, curved the long white scallop of Copacabana beach and beyond that the equally gentle curve of Ipanema. From here I could see the dark stain that marked the lake called Lagoa Rodrigo de Freitas—once an open bay but now partly drained and cut off from the sea by the strip of land and skyscrapers behind Ipanema beach. The western end of Ipanema, known as Leblon, was dominated by the peak of Dois Irmãos which reached down to the sea as a high, rocky headland. Beyond, hidden by the flat-topped peak of Gávea, lay the long sandy shoreline of Barra da Tijuca, where the city petered out into the wilderness known as the Baixada or lowlands of Jacarepaguá.

In the Glória district of central Rio, two men relax in a grove of 80-foot-high fig trees whose trunks and branches are veined with the roots of strangler vines.

Humming Modernity at the Jungle's Edge

PHOTOGRAPHS BY LOREN MCINTYRE

From the Atlantic, Rio presents its best profile, with Ipanema beach in the foreground, Copacabana to the right, and a tumble of dark mountains as a backdrop.

Rio is a uniquely deceptive city, humming with workaday energies in spite of a seaside façade that suggests whole-souled commitment to ease. The same waters that are a bather's or yachtsman's paradise lend themselves to a major fishing business, a sizable salt-producing industry, and a buoyant maritime trade (each year, upwards of 25 million tons of cargo are handled at the city's docks in the splendid natural harbour of Guanabara Bay). The residential high-rises that pack the Atlantic beachfront are rivalled by proliferating office towers in the city centre—headquarters for Brazil's chief financial institutions as well as its publishing concerns and broadcasting industry. As the aerial views on these pages make clear, Rio resembles St. Tropez and Chicago rolled into one—an unlikely hybrid that thrives on a mixture of work and pleasure.

Ships ride at anchor on either side of a bridge stretching five miles across Guanabara Bay. The span links Rio (background) to its sister city of Niterói.

An elevated expressway slices between the docks and Praça 15 de Novembro, a square (centre) named to mark the founding of the Brazilian Republic in 1889.

Evening lamps pick out the arched aqueduct that brought fresh water into 18th-Century Rio and now carries the last tramline through the modern city centre.

On the city's western margins, hillside and coastal developments — early stages in a massive new extension of Rio — nudge towards the flatlands of Jacarepaguá.

2

The Search for Living Space

Rio is a city of extremes, a place of violent and often shocking contrasts—between the virgin forests and the polluted streets, between the old quarters and the new, between primitive and civilized ways of life, between the rich and the poor. Most disturbing of all to an outsider are the widely different polarities of the human condition. I remember watching a man carefully make his bed one evening on a small patch of bare earth along one of the prosperous shopping streets of the city centre. Bed is too grand a word, for it consisted of no more than a tattered square of cloth laid out on the ground, yet the man was smoothing it down as if it were a silk sheet on a feathered mattress. What stuck in my mind about this scene was not so much the desperateness of the man's night lodging as the mauled state of his body. He was shoeless and stripped to the waist, and his back was lacerated with recent cuts four to six inches long. Presumably he had been in one of the knife fights that are common among the so-called *marginais*, or peripheral orders of society. On a wall above his head, like a Victorian bedside homily, was an exhortatory text from Rio's booming commercial world: *Um diamante é para sempre*—A diamond is forever.

Similar juxtapositions of affluence and poverty are to be found everywhere in Rio. You can see children begging for scraps of bread at the open-air cafés along Avenida Atlântica, grizzled beggars with fake blood-stained bandages in the smart shopping areas of Avenida Rio Branco, pathetic wretches on the park benches. In the Largo da Carioca, a large square in the city centre, beggar women squat on the pavement beneath the towering buildings of the big banks, where deals worth millions upon millions of dollars are done every day. One woman I met there was white, middle-aged, with blonde hair and blue eyes; she had once been beautiful, but now she was barefoot, ragged, dirty and worn. She told me she came into central Rio every day to beg. She lived in a room in the dormitory town of Santa Cruz, more than 30 miles away, and travelled back and forth every day by train. She did not actively solicit money, although I gave her some, and she was very happy that I talked to her. How she came to her present position she would not explain, but in Rio, where welfare payments are hard to obtain and in any case too small to live on, any ordinary accident of human existence can precipitate the steep slide into poverty—and the bottom is a long way down.

Equally, the top is a long way up. The upper class in Rio, drawn from the great landowning and industrial families of Brazil, is enormously wealthy. And during the boom years of the late 1960s and 1970s, the educated

Reduced to the merest speck by his awesome field of endeavour, a window-cleaner polishes the cylindrical façade of the 31-storey Hotel Naçional, by São Conrado beach in south-western Rio. Opened in the early 1970s, the hotel brought urban living to what had hitherto been an almost deserted seafront.

middle class not only expanded in size but gained impressively in prosperity. Businessmen, technocrats and executives in Brazil are paid salaries that often exceed those of their counterparts in North America. In their competition for the luxury homes in Rio, they have pushed up property values to such a level that a labourer on the minimum wage would have to work more than 300 years to earn the price of a seafront flat in Copacabana.

Many of the poor in Rio would count themselves lucky if they had a full-time job, let alone an apartment. Working-class Cariocas who have steady jobs tend to live in the northern suburbs, but a fifth of the population live in slum conditions, and many of them have to make do with a shanty in one of Rio's favelas. There are nearly 300 of these squatters' slums in Rio, more than in any other city in Brazil. The houses, built illegally on hillsides or swampland, generally consist of wood planks, mud, tin cans, corrugated iron and anything that comes to hand. Some cling to slopes so precipitous that the dwellings are in constant danger of being swept away in the heavy tropical rain storms that burst over the city. Not many years ago, several hundred favelados, as the inhabitants of the shanty towns are called, were killed in landslides and the authorities were forced to close the most dangerous favelas and shore up some of the others. With a few isolated exceptions, the favelas have no paved roads, no rubbish collection and no main drainage. Most favela houses are without running water, and some also lack electricity.

Even outside the favelas, the standard of living of the urban working class is low. The lack of main drainage and running water affects half the population. Of the sewage that does flow through main drains in greater Rio, 60 per cent is discharged, untreated, straight into Guanabara Bay, where the concentration of bacterial organisms has reached such a degree that bathing is unsafe. Nevertheless, an estimated 300,000 people use the waters of the bay for washing themselves and their clothes. Given such primitive levels of hygiene in Rio, and the poverty of so many of the people, it is not surprising that standards of health are low. Infant mortality is high and killer epidemics of meningitis are frequent. Although greater Rio has an average of 17 doctors for every 10,000 inhabitants—the best ratio in Brazil—nearly all of them work for fat fees in the South Zone.

The affluent sections of Rio may have adequate health care, but they are far from problem-free. This is especially true of the South Zone. For all its cachet of fashionable living, its millionaires, its luxury seafront apartments with bevies of servants, Copacabana has features of what one sociologist calls a super-slum. Only about 1 per cent of the built-up area is devoted to parks and gardens. The population density is one of the highest in any urban district in the world—more than 4,000 people per hectare, 10 times the maximum recommended by the World Health Organization. And in the narrow, congested back streets of Copacabana the noise of traffic can reach 125 decibels—equivalent to the close-

A caller is sheltered from the rain by one of Rio's distinctive telephone kiosks, nicknamed "Big Ears". Cariocas make heavy use of these ubiquitous phone booths, since the demand for home telephones far outstrips the supply.

quarters sound of a jet airliner taking off. (The noise limit recommended by the World Health Organization is 75 decibels.)

Throughout the downtown areas of Rio, the noise of traffic is almost equalled by the din of construction. The city is in a state of constant upheaval. When I was last there, more than half the arterial roads were closed for one reason or another, and cranes were busy everywhere on building sites. The new Metrô of Rio, constructed largely by the cut-and-cover method, burrows through the city's vital organs, devouring shops, trees, parks and streets with little regard for the sanctity of heritage or local sentiment. A skyscraper that was put up 10 years ago is considered old. Before long, it will be pulled down and replaced by a bigger and better one. There are, of course, enormous profits to be made from this headlong construction, and with the aid of speculators the process has advanced so fast that the average height of buildings in Rio has been rising by 10 floors a decade.

The pace of change in Rio is a result of the great social upheaval that has come with industrialization. Industrial development in Brazil did not begin until the 1870s, and its consequence—a massive growth of the urban population and a migration of people from the countryside—followed later still. But when it came, it was overwhelming. In the year 1900 the population of Rio was just over half a million. Twenty years later it had doubled. It doubled again in the next 20 years. In 1960 it was 3,500,000 and by the mid-1970s it had reached five million. A projection made by the United Nations Population Division has shown that if Rio's population continued to grow at its present rate, it would reach the staggering total of 19.4 million by the year 2000. By then, the world's largest city would be Mexico City, with 31.6 million, followed by Tokyo-Yokohama, São Paulo, New York and Calcutta, in that order. Rio would be in sixth place, with Shanghai and Bombay close behind in seventh and eighth place. Brazil would be the only country apart from India with two cities represented among the top eight.

Much of Rio's growth in the early years was due to a natural increase in the city's population and to immigration from European countries, especially Portugal, Italy and Spain. But during the agricultural depression in the 1930s, vast numbers of Brazilians poured into Rio from the rural districts of the country, especially the badlands of the north-east. Hungry, illiterate and diseased, the new arrivals saw Rio as a Shangri-La where life would be everlastingly sweet and bountiful and where all their ills would be cured. Most of them ended up in the favelas, which grew enormously as a result. By 1970 no less than 45 per cent of Rio's population consisted of people who had not been born there.

The constant population pressure and Rio's aspiration to modernize itself have had shattering effects on the fabric of the city. Urban history on the shore of Guanabara Bay is like archaeology speeded up. Whereas in Rome or even London, you can dig down and uncover layer after layer of buildings, each one representing several centuries, the layers in Rio—if you could find them after the pile-drivers have been at work—would represent only a few decades.

During the course of this century, two cities on the same site have all but disappeared. The first was the old colonial city that grew up in the 16th, 17th and 18th Centuries and survived, with later additions, until the beginning of the 20th Century. It carried with it most of the monuments of Rio's history: the original streets and houses on the Morro do Castelo, the churches, the mansions and palaces that embodied the Cariocas' spiritual and temporal aspirations. In a frenzied spate of rebuilding between 1900 and 1910, the colonial city was torn apart and replaced by the Rio of the so-called Belle Epoque, whose monumental splendour and florid decoration were modelled on the Paris of the Second Empire. Magnificent boulevards were laid out; libraries, theatres and grand public buildings embellished the city; whole districts were pulled down and rebuilt.

That city of the Belle Epoque can still be glimpsed here and there. Some of the municipal buildings have survived, notably the Municipal Theatre and the National Library. And in old suburbs like Catumbi and Estácio can still be found the era's characteristic small two-storeyed houses, with their balconies and coloured shutters, tiled façades and terracotta roofs. But much of the turn-of-the-century city has gone down under the assault of modern, high-rise development.

By the end of the 19th Century Rio had already spread out over the plains to the north, butted against the hills of Santa Teresa and the mountains of Tijuca in the west, and probed southwards to Botafogo Bay. As soon as tunnels were driven through to the South Zone from Botafogo—the first in 1892 and the second in 1904—the overflow from the North Zone rushed through to the uninhabited sand dunes of Copacabana and Ipanema, and the newly built Avenida Atlântica became lined with family houses.

But even this was not enough. The pressure of population was building up faster than extra land space could be provided. Unable to expand horizontally, Rio began to grow vertically. The first skyscraper went up in the city centre in 1925. By the 1940s, most of Copacabana had gone high-rise, and the Cariocas were already becoming a race of flat-dwellers. At the same time, the search for extra land continued. The front along Guanabara Bay was broadened twice, first in the 1920s with the earth from the Morro do Castelo and again in the 1960s with earth from the Morro de Santo Antônio. In 1969 it was the turn of Copacabana, where the Avenida Atlântica was widened to six lanes and extended out over the beach, which in turn was extended into the sea with dredged-up sand. From north to south and from east to west, new highways were built and

Pavement Geometry

Among the most notable ingredients of urban design in Rio are the broad mosaic pavements fringing the avenues and esplanades. The idea for these pavements came from Lisbon, where wave-patterned mosaics were laid to commemorate a great earthquake and flood that struck the city in 1755. Rio's builders, like Lisbon's, have elaborated on the originals, adding diamonds, squares and free-form shapes. Mosaics created around the turn of the century were usually made of inch-wide black and white stones; some of the latest variations employ larger stones in shades of grey or terra cotta.

The mosaics tend to be more pleasing in form than in function. Often laid without cement on a poorly prepared surface, they can be treacherous for pedestrians—full of cracks and potholes left by dislodged stones, and dangerously slippery when it is raining.

A new mosaic takes shape on a city-centre avenue.

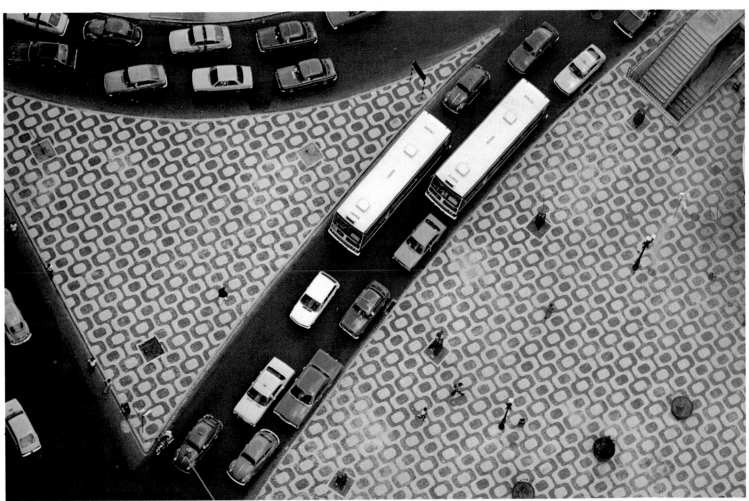

The pavements of the Avenida Rio Branco remain spacious, but many mosaics elsewhere are being eroded as roads are widened to accommodate Rio's traffic.

Next to a pattern of black and white squares, a disconcertingly three-dimensional mosaic begins. The illusion is achieved with stones of different shades of grey.

new tunnels bored. In 1968 the Rebouças tunnel provided a direct connection between the city centre and the Lagoa-Leblon district behind Ipanema, and three tunnels have been driven westward to open up a coastal motorway to the cities of Santos and São Paulo, providing access to the virgin flatlands beyond Ipanema-Leblon.

For all its efforts to modernize itself, Rio has been dealt one great disappointment. During the 1950s, many Brazilians took a hard look at the city and came to the conclusion that the old capital was nearing the end of its useful life. In their eyes, the mountains, the poor communications between zones, the overcrowding and the lack of space for unrestricted expansion disqualified Rio as a centre of government for the future. For a century or more, Brazilians had been toying with the idea of a new capital nearer the centre of this vast land, a city that would attract population and development away from the periphery. That idea finally came to fruition under President Juscelino Kubitschek, a physician from Minas Gerais, inland from Rio. Kubitschek had the vision and courage to construct the new capital city of Brasília—a spacious and dramatic array of superblocks—in the middle of the wild and empty central plateau of Brazil. The job was done in the incredibly short time of three years, one month and five days, counting from the selection of the master plan to the opening ceremony on April 21, 1960—an achievement that captured the imagination of the world and all but bankrupted the country.

On one of my visits to Rio, I had the good fortune to meet ex-President Kubitschek, not in Brasília but in Rio, where he had an elegant green and gold office suite at the top of the Manchete Building overlooking the Praia do Flamengo. From here I could look out over Guanabara Bay as far as Sugar Loaf in one direction and the Organ Mountains in the other. It was a blue and brilliant morning, and the splendour of the view prompted my first question. "Why, when you built Brasília, do you live in Rio?"

It was a mischievous question, but Kubitschek answered it patiently. He had the appearance and alertness of a man in his prime, although he was then over 70. He also seemed a very nice man. I could see why he could persuade a nation to build a city. He possessed not just charm but a patently genuine likeableness: people would be happy to do things for him.

He replied: "You might as well ask why, since I was born in Minas, I don't live there. As a matter of fact I do live in Brasília. I have a farm near there and I go there weekends and as often as I can. I go into Brasília just to see it, to feel it, to breathe that air, and I am happy."

"But it is a fact, isn't it," I asked him, "that the planes to Rio are full every Friday evening with people who work in Brasília and can't wait to get back to Rio for the weekend?"

"There may be such people," he said. "Rio is Rio. With all its beaches and parks, it will always be a magnet. But you must remember that

Workmen install a drainage pipe near one end of the Frei Caneca Tunnel shortly before its opening in 1977. Burrowing 960 feet through a mountain, the artery links the city centre with growing communities to the west. More than a dozen tunnels have been built in Rio since the first one was completed in 1892.

Brasília is becoming a mature city in its own right. Its population has passed the million mark, and many of those people were born there. Brasília is their home town and they look to the future in the interior. They don't want to escape to Rio.

"To be sure," he added, "Rio has problems. I believe that they can be solved. As the interior of Brazil opens up, immigration to Rio will decline. But you should speak to Lúcio Costa. He was the architect who designed Brasília. He is now designing a new Rio. You should speak to him."

As I was leaving, ex-president Kubitschek called me back. He was writing on the title page of a book he had just published called *Porque Construí Brasília* ("Why I Built Brasília"). "To my dear friend Douglas Botting," he wrote. Not long afterwards, on the road between São Paulo and Rio, his car came into collision with a lorry. The man who had built Brasília was killed instantly.

Lúcio Costa is a member of a brilliant generation of Brazilian architects, among them Oscar Niemeyer, whose work in urban design during the 1940s and 1950s aroused world-wide excitement. Costa and his colleagues owed much to the concepts of Le Corbusier, the French architect who was one of the leaders of the Modern Movement, and also to the structural possibilities of reinforced concrete and steel. In the bold and still controversial public buildings of Brasília, their ideas achieved their most monumental consummation. Now, it seemed, Lúcio Costa was to do for the old capital what he had done for the new. He had been commissioned to plan and direct the building of a huge extension to Rio in the Baixada de Jacarepaguá, the flatlands of sandbars, salt lagoons and bush country that are now within 10 minutes' drive of Ipanema and Leblon, along the new coastal motorway to the west.

I first met Lúcio Costa in an office in a skyscraper that he had designed himself—the glass-and-concrete Ministry of Education and Health building in the city centre, the first truly modern building in South America, erected between 1938 and 1943. It is one of the ironies of contemporary monumental architecture, however, that even the most avant-garde designs of today are sometimes inappropriate to the unforeseen contingencies of tomorrow. The building was given louvred sunbreakers to keep out the direct rays of the tropical sun, but it did not have double glazing to keep out the traffic din, the level of which had never been imagined when the edifice was put up. I simply could not hear what Lúcio Costa was saying to me. We therefore arranged to meet again in his planning office in the Baixada.

Roughly the shape of a triangle, with the mountains looming behind and the 12-mile beach of the Barra da Tijuca ranged in front, the Baixada de Jacarepaguá is an important part of the Rio backlands. In the middle of this wilderness, the new extension of Rio will eventually house some 3,500,000 extra Cariocas.

I had already seen the initial development at the Baixada de Jacarepaguá, and I could not honestly say I liked it. It looked like an abandoned rocket-launching site. Beyond a jumble of bungalows and club houses rose the outlines of three astonishing round towers. Two of them were unfinished and skeletal—gaunt columns of steel whose vertical tumescence seemed to rape the horizontal harmony of the plain. They were the remnants of an Oscar Niemeyer plan that had envisaged several clusters of residential towers arranged like flowers on the tendrils of a vine. The project had run into trouble, gone broke and been abandoned. After the fiasco, Lúcio Costa's planning group had been appointed to exert some control over the development.

Lúcio Costa was a merry, good humoured man with twinkling eyes, a curly moustache and a very Carioca sense of humour. He was bright and active, and I was taken aback when he told me that he had been a pupil at the Royal Grammar School in Newcastle, England, and had left just before the First World War. I had got his age wrong by almost 20 years.

I suggested to him that it was a tragedy to build a new city here at all.

"I agree. But it is absolutely inevitable. No power on earth can stop it happening. And since it is inevitable, it is better to do it in a controlled way, preserving as much as we can of the beauties of the region."

What had made it inevitable were the new tunnels and the new highway to Santos and São Paulo. The road provided easy access from the city centre, and the pressure of population was already pushing new building development into the Baixada.

"Brasília had a rigid plan," Lúcio Costa explained to me. "This has a fluid one. In Brazil it is sometimes better to have no plan at all than one

Vigorously pursued by would-be passengers, two ancient electric cars journey between the city centre and the suburb of Santa Teresa— the only tram route that has survived into an age of buses. In Rio, trams are called bondes, a nickname that goes back to the 1860s, when the printed tickets for the first mule-drawn trams reminded Cariocas of government bonds.

that cannot be changed. In this case I envisage three outlying urban areas, one in each corner of the triangle, and the future metropolitan centre of Rio in the middle. I am proposing that the centre should consist of 70-storey blocks, but the rest of the development will be low-density, with lots of green areas, lots of space, and an undeveloped seafront. A place for people to come, you see. There will be industry up here in the hills, low-income housing over here, nature reserves down here by the lagoons. We will turn building sites into oases planted with almond and cashew and coconut trees."

He leapt up and down to get charts and drawings from filing cabinets. On the sheets of paper were plans of residential compounds, front elevations, domestic interiors, vistas of palm trees, lines of access roads, broad ideas and minute details. It was very exciting—but sad all the same.

"Only heaven—and the government—knows how it will turn out," Costa said. "We do what we can. People ask what it will be like in the year 2000. The year 2000 is tomorrow." He looked out of the window over the plains to the blue mountains. There were signs up everywhere: "NOVA IPANEMA. 540 APTS. ALL SOLD", "NOVA LEBLON", "WIMBLEDON PARK. ALL LOTS SOLD".

"Fortunately," he said, turning round to me again, eyes twinkling, "I will be dead."

No man has protested against the destruction of Rio's natural landscape more vehemently than Burle Marx, Brazil's leading landscape gardener. He designed the gardens on the Flamengo waterfront and the patterned mosaics of the pavements along the Avenida Atlântica in Copacabana, as well as big municipal gardens in Brasília and São Paulo. Burle Marx has a country home on the way to Guaratiba, in the next bay beyond Jacarepaguá. At weekends, he has open house, so one Saturday morning I drove out to have lunch with him and talk about the fate of the city.

His home turned out to be an old farm-house, with its own 17th-Century chapel next door. From a covered verandah that ran the whole length of the front of the house, there was a magnificent view of green lawns and açaí palms and tropical shrubbery stretching towards the plains and the forested mountains beyond. After the noise and frenzy of Rio, it was a wonderfully quiet place. Quiet, that is, except for the powerful operatic aria that issued from the interior of the house. Senhor Marx was singing at the piano.

My arrival was announced and the aria came to an abrupt stop. Burle Marx appeared on the verandah. He had shoulder-length white hair and a clipped white moustache and old blue jeans. He absent-mindedly poured me half a pint of neat rum and motioned me to sit down.

"I came to Rio when I was five years old," he told me, "and I have lived here most of my life. In the 1920s and 1930s it was truly a beautiful city. But now I can't stand it."

I asked him why.

"I can remember Copacabana when it had hardly any houses on it. Now look at it: skyscrapers, pollution, overcrowding, noise, traffic. It is unbearable. All of Rio is becoming like that now. Out of stupidity or cupidity, or both, they are pulling down big skyscrapers to build even bigger skyscrapers, they are cutting down trees, tearing up gardens, covering everything in concrete. In minutes, a bulldozer can destroy the work of centuries. Only the most drastic measures can prevent not just Rio but the whole of Brazil from being turned into a desert. The Botanical Gardens were once the biggest in the world, now they are reduced to a fifth of their original size. Brazilians, you see, are frightened of plants, frightened of nature."

We went into lunch. In the dining-room was an aquarium full of angel fish, *acarás* and bleeding hearts. A glass cabinet held a large collection of old paintings, Brazilian carvings and effigies of saints from old churches. Burle Marx was clearly impassioned about his country's heritage.

"We are throwing it all away as if it were worthless. You know, Brazil bought the defoliant chemicals that the U.S. Army used in Vietnam: they used them to destroy the forests in the Amazon and Mato Grosso to create farmland. They would have destroyed the Tijuca Forest as well and turned it into a big new property development if it hadn't been made into a national park. Not that that means anything. Anyone can get round the law here. We need a law to respect the law."

We finished our lunch and went out to see Senhor Marx's unique garden—200 acres containing 3,000 different species of tropical plants

Located in the centre of Rio, the New Cathedral imitates in steel and concrete the blunt-topped form of ancient Mayan pyramids in Mexico's Yucatan.

Shapes of the Future

Rio is a city that looks to the future, and avant-garde construction is one of its specialities. In the 1940s, architects came from all over the world to see new rectilinear office blocks that put the city in the forefront of the Modern Movement. Although the new capital of Brasília stole the limelight in the 1950s and 1960s, Rio's tradition of innova-tive building was kept alive by a series of bold projects, among them the New Cathedral (above), whose site was created by the levelling of Santo Antônio hill. The earth from the hill was used, in turn, to form a waterfront park—the setting for a space-age war memorial (overleaf) that won instant recognition as an architectural landmark.

An angular rival to Sugar Loaf, in the background, this stone prism in Flamengo Park at the edge of Guanabara Bay commemorates Estácio de Sá, Rio's founder.

Surrounded by street lights, Rio's memorial to the dead of the Second World War seems to float above the time-exposure streaks of Flamengo Park traffic.

The jumbled shacks of a favela—a shanty town built by squatters—spill down the side of Dona Marta hill to the very edge of a middle-class district below.

inside the bedroom, hidden by a plywood partition, is a ceramic lavatory that can be flushed with a bucket of water. Since the favela does not have main drainage, I assume these householders have dug their own soak-aways. The house is desperately overcrowded, but by favela standards it is remarkably well equipped with consumer durables: apart from the electrical goods in the bedroom there is a gas stove and a big refrigerator in the kitchen. These items were all acquired second-hand, but there are two brand new bikes leaning against the outside wall.

"The thatch-roofed verandah is festooned with laundry. All around the outside of the house lies an immense amount of rubbish—old tins, bottles, rags, litter of all kinds. It is surprising what a seemingly large proportion of Rio's rubbish the favela people, with their low purchasing power, are able to produce. Rocinha is strewn all over with great stinking, spreading dumps. But then, there is no one to take it away and nowhere else to put it.

"House No. 2 is near the top of the favela. It is a wood-framed structure perched on a steep slope and propped up at the front on stilts. A slippery mud path leads up to the house, and a flight of ramshackle steps composed of scraps of wood nailed together at crazy angles reaches up to the door. A wicker cage containing a yellow-breasted, black-eyed songbird hangs by the door, and the ubiquitous laundry is suspended from a clothes line at the back. There are two rooms and a kitchen and a house-proud domestic atmosphere inside, with cloths covering the tables and various ornaments neatly arranged for their decorative effect. The house cost $160. Six people live in it: the father, who earns more than $80 a month as a hospital porter; the mother, who brings in another $50 as a shop assistant in a bakery in the Tijuca district; three children aged nine, seven and five; and the mother-in-law.

"The mother-in-law is Bahian, but she has lived in the Rocinha favela for 23 years. Her son and daughter-in-law joined her here six years ago. Things have not improved much in that time, the mother-in-law tells me. Still, the family is clearly an aspiring one. All the children will receive an education. The youngest, a boy, won first prize a few years ago in the Rio de Janeiro Beautiful Baby Contest, organized by the evening paper *Última Hora*. The father proudly produces a framed newspaper photo of his little Omar when he was the bonniest baby of Rio. Clearly they are determined that their children should do better than the majority of favela children. They are very courteous people and when I prepare to leave, they give me a present—a little ashtray—and will not accept any remonstrances from me about it."

For a place so crammed with human beings, Rocinha is a relatively rural favela, overlooking the sea and green, undeveloped mountainside. By comparison, Mangueira—the next favela I visited—is thoroughly urban, looking towards the Maracanã football stadium, the zoo and the busy shipping zone of Guanabara Bay. The correct name for Mangueira

Two boys from a favela take a pavement seat outside a downtown store for a multi-screen view of the night's programmes. Although the cramped homes of Rio's shanty towns often have television sets, many favela children like to spend the evenings roaming through the city in search of amusements.

is Telegraph Hill, but it is popularly known as Mangueira because the central railway station at the foot of the hill is called Estação Primeira de Mangueira, after a *mangueira* or mango tree that used to grow there. Today the inhabitants refer to the place as the *morro*, or hill, rather than as the favela of Mangueira, but the distinction is academic.

I was taken around Mangueira by a Senhor Antonito, a very dignified and upright old black man who had lived in the favela for 50 years and was now one of its most respected elders. Like Rocinha, the place was a confusion of multicoloured shacks, corrugated iron, bare-foot children, pigs, dogs, kites flying, and washing fluttering on an infinite network of clothes lines. Everywhere I could smell the stench of sewage. Nowhere could I see a single right angle: shanties had been erected without recourse to plumb line or carpenter's spirit level, and they leaned at all angles, door-ways and window frames askew. Some houses were detached, others were in an accretive relationship to each other, one family's back wall some-times serving as the neighbours' side wall.

For all the rampant disarray, I was aware of a much more tightly knit, more self-respecting community here than at Rocinha. At the foot of the hill was the Samba Palace—the headquarters and rehearsal centre of the famous Mangueira Samba School, one of those great institutions of Rio that are not schools at all but Carnival clubs with thousands of members who parade through the city in the great pre-Lenten celebration. A tarmac street ran up the hill, and near the top was a medical post, a school and a Protestant church founded by missionaries.

"Everything we have here," remarked Senhor Antonito proudly, "is a result of our own efforts. The people have paid for everything—the running water, the electric lights. The government has paid for nothing. We even run our own health insurance scheme. How else could we afford to see a doctor?"

I was warmly received at every turn. Senhor Antonito shouted to the children: "Come and show the foreigner how courteous you can be!" and they came and touched my hand. A little girl said, "You will come back, won't you?" At a little wooden stall doing a busy trade in small things—black plug tobacco, confectionery, green vegetables—I bought some beer for Senhor Antonito and sweets for the children.

For the ordinary self-respecting and aspiring people of the favelas, life is often complicated by the state of war that exists between the favela-based criminals on the one hand and the police on the other. Only a week before I visited the Mangueira favela, a force of 200 policemen armed with machine-guns made a lightning dawn raid and arrested 60 criminal suspects on the grounds that they had no identity documents. One of them was a taxi-driver who was seized before he could get his documents out of the glove box of his taxi. He happened to be the son of a famous inhabitant of Mangueira, the legendary musician Cartola, who had founded the great Mangueira Samba School back in the 1930s. When Cartola and his no less famous wife, Zica, came to their son's assistance, Cartola was kicked and Zica was almost thrown into a patrol wagon. Only the intervention of friends known to the police saved one of Brazil's most respected popular composers from being imprisoned as a common felon.

From the late 1950s to the early 1970s, the warfare between police and criminals made Rio look like Chicago in the 1930s. Robberies ranging from pickpocketing to armed bank raids were an everyday occurrence, and nearly a thousand murders were committed annually, most of which went unsolved. The police, frustrated by the failure of ordinary law enforcement procedures, took the law into their own hands and simply wiped out petty criminals and minor favela gangsters through the agency of a secret, off-duty organization called the *Esquadrão da Morte*, or Death Squad. The squad would mark down a known criminal for elimination without trial, pick him up from his favela at night, drive him to a lonely spot on some deserted road, strip him, bind him, torture him and then shoot him as many as a hundred times. They would attach a piece of paper to the corpse with a skull and crossbones drawn on it, the initials E.M., and a statement such as "I was a car thief", "I was a marijuana pedlar", or "I was planning to rob a bank". The Death Squad would then depart, and later their "public relations" man, who became known as *Rosa Vermelha* (Red Rose)—a reference to the blossoming of blood from the exit hole of a bullet wound—would telephone the crime desks of various newspapers with details of where the body could be found. It was his grisly custom to call the body a *presunto* (ham) if it was a white man and a *chouriço* (smoked sausage) if it was a black man.

The Death Squad was at one time reckoned to account for as many as 200 of the unsolved murders in Rio every year, although it later became evident that some of these murders were the results of gang warfare between rival favela-based criminal syndicates. Eventually, a public outcry led to official investigations that curtailed the activities of the Death Squad. But the culprits were never brought to trial.

While I was at Mangueira I witnessed a cruel little incident that summed up for me the roughness of life in the favelas. I watched a gang of youths set upon a young black man who was clearly both drunk and ill. I asked who he was and what was wrong with him. A bystander told me that although he was a clever person who could read and write, he was mentally disordered in some way, and when he drank alcohol he became mad. The youths bullied him mercilessly. They barged into him and elbowed him and boxed his ears. Finally they pulled his trousers down around his ankles so that he stumbled and fell on his back, where he lay indecently exposed to the casual scrutiny of a group of women who had arrived to attend a committee meeting of the Mangueira Samba School.

Senhor Antonito took me to one side. "You may not think so, but life is better here now. When I came here in 1926, the street was just a rut in the ground and you had to go right down to the bottom of the hill with a pail on your head to get water. We have a bit more money now, more mobility. I am a Carioca from the yolk of the egg. I was born in Copacabana when it was just sand and you could buy 20 square metres of it for almost nothing. I remember the days when there were no motor cars and you had to wear a collar and tie to ride on a tram. Now Rio has become the leading city of the world."

I looked down the hill towards the up-and-coming middle-class suburbs of Grajaú and Andaraí beneath the Tijuca hills. How long, I wondered, before the speculators turned their eyes towards these favela hills, with their convenient locations and their splendid views? As if he read my thoughts, Senhor Antonito went on: "The government say they are going to redevelop the Mangueira favela. I think all they will do is expose the land to property speculators. Where can I go if I have to move now?"

It is quite true that plans are afoot to redevelop the favelas. To higher orders of Rio society, favelas are eyesores. Their inhabitants are parasites on the city—and likely converts to political extremism. The government has set a target date of the late 1980s for the eradication of the favelas, and some have been removed already. Their inhabitants have been rehoused in low-cost suburbs on the extreme outskirts of Rio, far from the jobs and excitement of the big city that drew them and their parents and grandparents from the countryside in the first place. If the plan is carried through to its conclusion, Rio will be a better place to look at—but not necessarily a better place to live in. The city's ills run deep, and whether Rio will ever find a human stability to match the enduring beauty of its natural setting remains very much an open question.

Hovels on the Hills

Lines of washing add a splash of colour to favela homes, whose haphazard construction sometimes conceals an unexpected degree of interior comfort and order.

Clinging to steep hillsides throughout the city, the favelas of Rio are among the world's most conspicuous slums. In these motionless avalanches of squalor live hundreds of thousands of squatters, most of them deeply impoverished—yet notably resourceful as well. Their shacks, built of anything from scraps of wood to bricks accumulated a few at a time, are a triumph of ingenuity over sites rejected by town planners as unusable. In the absence of service mains, the residents manage to provide themselves with water, rudimentary drainage, and electricity—often supplied to a single householder who distributes it to the district and acts as bill-collector. Considering the hardships and uncertainties of their lives, the favelados—as the illegal hill-dwellers are called—display a sense of community and organization that is nothing short of remarkable.

A woman looks on as two youngsters concoct a game in a tiny yard. On average, children in favelas receive only a single year of schooling.

On her way to get water for the household, a girl descends steps that were built by the squatters themselves.

At a public fountain—perhaps illegally connected to the municipal supply by the favela residents—a young woman labours over her washing.

A boy helps hang out the day's wash. Taking in laundry from prosperous middle-class districts near by is one of the few jobs available to the favela women.

A favelado climbs homewards with the family shopping, passing a house with an improvised water system.

A boy flies his kite from a rooftop where a loudspeaker has been installed by the community to broadcast samba music to the whole district.

Sunshine reaching into a windowless home lights a seamstress's work and illuminates a picture on a wall.

A proud father and his mother-in-law hold up family photographs and a certificate declaring that the youngest child won a Beautiful Baby contest (page 54).

With varying degrees of co-operativeness, children interrupt their afternoon games and assemble for a group portrait in front of a multicoloured favela façade.

3

Sugar and Gold, Colonists and Kings

People in Rio often speak wistfully of a Golden Age, some idealized period in the city's past when all was beauty, charm and perfection, when the world of man was in harmony with the world of nature, when life was one long, voluptuous dream. Implicit in this nostalgia is a feeling among Cariocas that during the 20th-Century frenzy of urban change, something has gone wrong, some essential quality of Rio has been lost or betrayed. When did this idealized Rio finally cease to exist? Was it in the building boom after the Second World War when whole districts of the old city were demolished? Was it in the 1930s, when the 100-yard-wide Avenida Presidente Vargas was driven for two and a half miles through the centre of Rio, destroying more than 500 houses? Or was it in the 1920s, when the nucleus of the original city on the Morro do Castelo was razed?

These and other dates are sometimes cited by Cariocas; but to my mind, the essential Rio is not tied to any particular time. It is a distillation of the struggles and achievements of the city's entire history—four centuries that brought Rio from a fortified outpost on the rim of an unknown continent to its present status as one of the biggest cities in Latin America, four centuries that transformed its population from a handful of hard-bitten colonists into a richly varied society quite unlike any other. Throughout that long span were forged the qualities that more and more Cariocas believe to have been overwhelmed by the turmoil of the 20th Century, but that seem to me, on closer consideration, more difficult to extinguish than they fear.

The city they cherish—and Brazil as a whole—got off to a slow start. The fleeting visits of Portuguese explorers at the beginning of the 16th Century had suggested that the new-found land would be something less than a boon to the hard-up royal treasury of Portugal. Instead of gold, rubies and pearls, the early explorers found only monkeys, parrots and brazilwood— the *pau-brasil* (so called because the red colour of the wood resembles a live coal or *brasa*) from which the country took its name. Brazil was therefore left largely to itself, visited only by a few merchants trading in brazilwood logs, which yielded an excellent red dye. When Portugal eventually established colonial settlements in the 1530s and 1540s, the sites chosen were far to the north and south of Rio.

It was the French and the Dutch who filled the vacuum left by the Portuguese. Disinclined to accept the territorial claims made by the discoverers of the New World, they energetically disputed Portuguese rights for many years. In 1555 the French decided to add to their empire

A tiled panel in a Rio hotel shows slaves spreading out coffee beans to dry in the sun, while their masters supervise from the shade. In the early 19th Century, slave-based coffee production on outlying plantations helped transform Rio from a torpid colonial outpost into a prosperous trading city with paved streets, hotels, banks and European-style shops.

a large part of southern Brazil, which would be called Antarctic France. To this end, Admiral Nicolas Durand de Villegaignon set sail with three ships and 600 men for Guanabara Bay, where he built a fortress on a small island called Sergipe, later renamed Villegaignon and today occupied by Brazil's naval school. Alarmed, the Portuguese attempted to dislodge the settlers. The fortress-headquarters of Antarctic France survived one attack in 1560, mounted by the Governor-General of Brazil, Mem de Sá, from Bahia, Brazil's first capital city, a thousand miles away to the north. Five years later, an expedition under the governor's energetic young nephew, Estácio de Sá, was dispatched from Portugal with instructions to drive out the French settlers once and for all and establish a permanent Portuguese presence in Guanabara Bay.

On March 1, Estácio's party landed on a small beach beside the entrance to the bay, under the rocky scarp of Sugar Loaf mountain. At this un-promising spot, they built a moated, mud-and-wattle fort and pronounced the foundation of the city of São Sebastião do Rio de Janeiro—the city's official name to this day. The name Sebastião was chosen in honour of the infant king of Portugal, Dom Sebastião. As part of the founding ceremony a statue of the king's own namesake, St. Sebastian, was brought ashore and placed in a small thatched chapel. (This image now stands in the Church of São Sebastião at Tijuca, a hill suburb to the west of the original site.)

Two years passed before the Portuguese were finally able to drive the French from their well-defended positions in the interior of the bay. In early January, 1567, Mem de Sá unexpectedly arrived with reinforcements from Bahia, and on January 20—a day still celebrated as a public holiday in Rio—Estácio de Sá led his troops against the enemy's fortifications. Estácio, bare-chested and fearless, fought in the front line with his men, a clear target for Indian sharp-shooters fighting alongside the French. With the battle nearly won, he was shot in the face by a poison arrow and fell, mortally wounded. A month later the founder of the city of São Sebastião do Rio de Janeiro died of his wounds.

After the death of Estácio, Mem de Sá assumed command. Now that the French had been expelled and their Indian allies demoralized, he could transfer the settlement to a site that was less restricted than the narrow beach of Estácio's original fort. On March 1, the Portuguese abandoned the so-called Old City below Sugar Loaf and removed them-selves a few miles north to a low, strategically placed hill—Morro do Castelo—along the shore of the bay.

The space of a whole lifetime had elapsed since the discovery of the bay; but an even longer period was to pass before Rio rose to any real im-portance. Initially it served little purpose for the Portuguese government in Brazil. The existing towns of Bahia and Olinda in the north, and São Paulo and São Vicente in the south, overshadowed it both administratively and economically. Although Rio had one of the finest natural harbours in

In the mid-16th Century, the sole settlers in the locality of Rio were French colonists who chose to ignore Portugal's prior territorial claims. This contemporary French map dramatizes a Portuguese armada's abortive attempt in 1560 to dislodge them from island fortifications near the mouth of Guanabara Bay. Five years later, a second eviction force drove the French from the bay and laid the foundations of the present-day city.

the world, its surroundings of jungle-clad mountains or marshy flatlands were abominable to settle and develop. The energies of Rio in its early years were thus mainly expressed in stern pioneering endeavour. Palm tree by palm tree, swamp by swamp, the early colonists conquered the Sertão, the backlands, and overcame the hostile wilderness, the great distances, the heat and the teeming insects.

The Portuguese in Brazil, arriving without women of their own, were very partial to the naked Indian women, and soon learned to make love in a swaying hammock. In this way, in spite of their small numbers, the settlers of Rio were able to populate the country with their mixed-blooded offspring, the caboclos—the first line of native-born pioneers who opened up the hinterland. In 1585 Rio had a population of 150 white people. By 1600 the number of whites had increased to 750, but there were 3,000 Indians or half-breeds, and a hundred black slaves. The slaves were imported to replace the Indian men, who—because they came from a pre-agricultural society—proved totally unsuited to agrarian labour. Before long the Indians died or were driven away.

Even with this modest population, the Morro do Castelo was proving cramped. Since the Indians no longer posed any threat, there was no

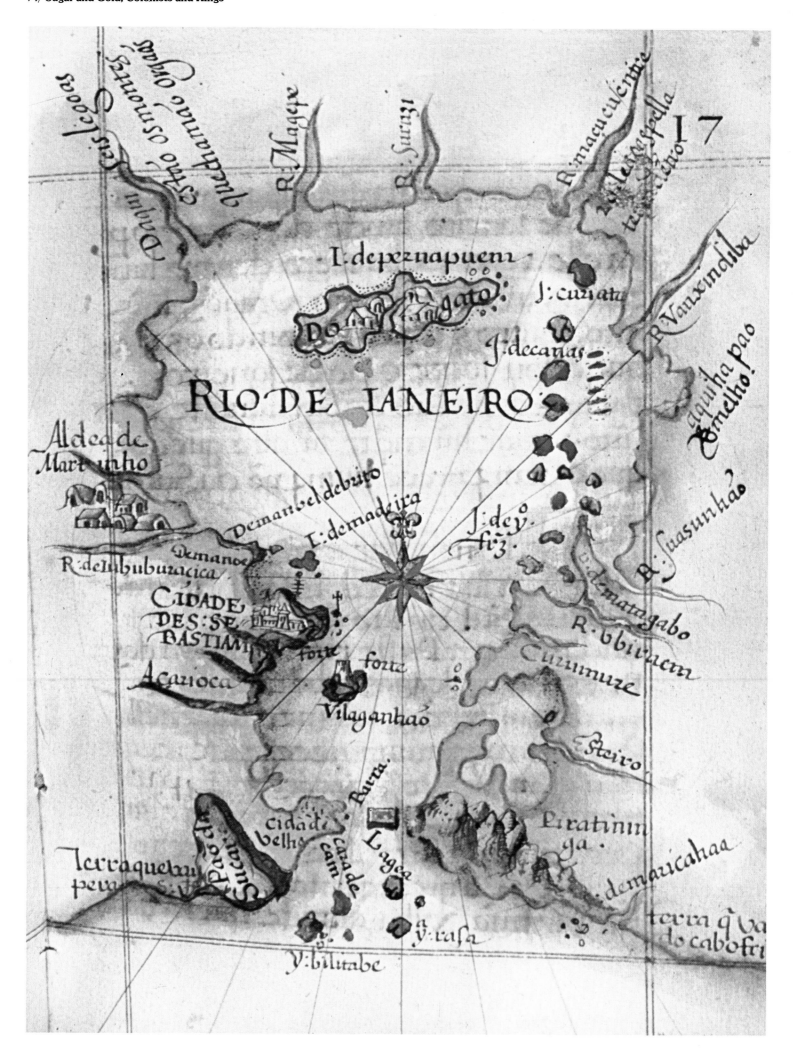

The earliest Portuguese map of Guanabara Bay, profusely endowed with compass lines, was drawn in the late 1570s by the royal cartographer, Luís Teixeira. He abbreviated the name of the newly founded city of São Sebastião do Rio de Janeiro to "Cidade des Sebastiam" and drew the largest island in the bay—Ilha do Governador as it is known today—with its first few sugar mills.

reason why the Cariocas should continue to live huddled together within mud ramparts on the hill. Gradually they began to move down to the adjacent shore where the beach served as a street and the canoes that were used for communication with outlying farms and plantations could be landed in front of their owners' houses. Slowly, a row of houses grew along the shoreline in the direction of the hill now called São Bento. Behind those houses grew a second line, and behind the second, a third.

By the early 17th Century, the little town occupied a rectangle of flat, dry land bounded by four hills—the Castelo, São Bento, and two others named Santo Antônio and Conceição. Some of the first streets laid down in this original rectangle—such as the Rua São José and Rua do Ouvidor—still follow the course they were given then. The compact streets and the narrow alleys of the town were muddy and pot-holed, with gutters down the middle where rain water flowed or stagnated. For long periods each year the little city was flooded and the people could catch crabs at the bottom of their gardens. The higgledy-piggledy houses were mostly mean, low and dark, built of lath and mud, without glass in the windows and poorly furnished (much like the houses of frontier settlements deep within Brazil today). The Cariocas lived on fish and whales harpooned in the bay, along with foods the Indians had taught them to eat—notably the staple *farinha de mandioca*, the dry flour prepared from cassava tubers. The only regular source of fresh water was the little Rio Carioca, and the only means of getting it into the city was in buckets on the heads of slaves. Every so often the population was reduced by epidemics of smallpox.

Rio's amusements were distinctly limited. Brawling in the streets evidently provided one kind of diversion: in 1637 a visiting cleric from Lima, in Peru, described the inhabitants as so unruly that they killed one another "as if they were bedbugs". Church-going provided another distraction. Founded as it was by solidly Catholic Portugal, Rio was abundantly endowed with ecclesiastical buildings, including an array of splendid edifices raised on the summits of the hills by the various Catholic orders—the Jesuit College and Church on the Morro do Castelo (built in 1583), the Franciscan Convent and Church on Santo Antônio (1615), the Benedictine Monastery on São Bento (1628). The oldest surviving church, Nossa Senhora do Cabeça, dates from this time; it was built in 1625 on the north side of Lagoa Rodrigo de Freitas, near the present Rua Faro.

As the 17th Century progressed, Rio began to develop as a port. What kept the port busy initially was the shipping of sugar. Sugar cane grew well in the plantations of the great estates along the coast and fetched a very high price as a luxury in Europe. Thus the Portuguese were able to provide an economic base in Brazil for the first permanent modern tropical society in the world. A country that had seemed good for nothing but dyewood and souls soon developed into a plantation colony based on the *engenhos*, or sugar mills, and the *casas-grandes*, the big houses of the great patriarchal families who owned most of the land. In the mid-17th Century, when Dutch military action disrupted the export of sugar from north-eastern Brazil, Rio became a prime sugar producing area.

A second step towards Rio's economic prominence was the discovery, in 1695, of gold some hundreds of miles inland, in the area that became the state of Minas Gerais (General Mines). A dirt road was built linking the mines to Rio, which became the gateway for miners and supplies flowing into the prospecting fields, and the conduit for gold flowing back to the royal treasury in Portugal.

With the growing prosperity of Rio came a massive expansion of African slavery. First on the plantations and then in the mines, the demand for labour grew insatiably, and Rio soon became one of the chief slave importing cities in Brazil. No one knows how many slaves were landed in a particular year or even decade, but the numbers were colossal. In Brazil as a whole, somewhere between 500,000 and 600,000 Africans came in during the 17th Century—equivalent to at least a third of the colony's total population. And with the boom in mining, imports during the 18th Century reached two million at the very least. Black slaves easily outnumbered white colonists by the beginning of the 19th Century.

The large number of Africans in Rio transformed the physiognomy of the people. The white men of the city had no inhibitions about sleeping with slave girls. In the matter of race and sex, the Portuguese never displayed the same reserve as their colonial rivals, the Dutch, British, French. From the 8th to the 13th Century, the people of Portugal had been subject to a darker race more powerful and sophisticated than themselves—the Moors of North Africa—and they had been in contact with the peoples of the West African coast ever since the late 15th Century. Their sexual ideal was the plump, dark-skinned woman, who often became their concubine. So great was the need to populate the country that Church and society looked the other way. All procreation was greatly appreciated.

From the union of black slaves and white colonists in Rio came a large mixed population, neither European nor African but native to the land in which they were born. Many, being born of slave mothers, were slaves themselves. But some owners would free their half-white offspring and also the black mothers who bore them, so that there soon appeared a substantial non-white free population. Thus, while the vast majority of blacks were slaves, there was no necessary correlation between being black and being a slave. By the 18th Century, many people of mixed parentage and more than a few ex-slaves were slave-owners themselves.

The cultural influence of the Africans in Rio was enormous. White Cariocas were reared in intimate contact with black people. Blacks were their wet-nurses, their nursery story-tellers, their childhood playmates, often their first sexual contacts, their confidants, their mistresses, their

"Independence or death!" was the cry of the Prince Regent Dom Pedro, who in 1822 declared Brazil free from Portuguese colonial rule and crowned himself its Emperor. In these contemporary illustrations, he is seen wearing his ceremonial vestments (above), and accepting the acclamation of the citizens of Rio in the Campo de Santana (right).

right-hand men. The chief black servant of slave-owning households gained a status only a little lower than that of her white mistress; and a nanny who had brought up a white child would often remain the most important and trusted person in his or her life.

As a result, nothing in Rio was untouched by African customs, beliefs, and behaviour. The Africans were vivacious, extrovert, festive and non-violent people. They adored bright colours and audacious clothes and extravagant hats; under their influence, Rio came to have a more and more animated and light-hearted aspect. They created a more rhythmic kind of Brazilian music, they helped develop Carnival along its present lines, they softened and enriched the Portuguese language of Brazil, they relaxed the austerity and enlivened the festivals of the Catholic religion, and they introduced the religion of their own spiritist cults. They also provided some distinctive elements of Brazilian cuisine. During the centuries that the slave ships travelled between the two continents, many African herbs, spices and fruits came to Brazil, and with these ingredients the slaves modified Portuguese and Indian dishes to suit their own palate. They introduced hot peppers and *dendê* oil, okra, ginger, coconut, crushed melon and pumpkin seeds, and they continued the African practice of roasting food wrapped in leaves. Since it was the black cook who ruled the kitchen of the great houses, African recipes inevitably found their way into the cuisine of society as a whole.

In physical as well as cultural terms, Rio underwent major alterations during the 18th Century. The age of the Amerindian wattle hut gave way to an age of stone houses boasting several floors, latticed balconies and tiled roofs. More and more churches sprang up, built out of local or imported stone and ornamented with wrought marble and carved wood. Lakes and swamps were drained, and gardens and promenades were laid out over them. A palace was built for the governor in the Largo do Paço (now the Praça 15 de Novembro), the waterfront square that was the focal point of the city's life. Fresh water was brought into the centre of the city in 1750 by canalizing the Carioca River over a splendid Roman-style aqueduct, 886 feet long and 210 feet high—still one of the outstanding landmarks in Rio. At its fountain terminus, a policeman was always on duty to control the disorderly crowds of slaves who queued up with buckets there.

The growing prosperity of Rio in the 17th and early 18th Centuries was followed by a rise in political status. At various times during the 17th Century the Cariocas acquired new administrative responsibilities and won greater powers over the southern and western areas of the colony. During the 18th Century, the city's significance was greatly increased by a new strategic consideration. North-east Brazil was no longer threatened by the Dutch, but the Portuguese were now struggling with the Spanish for the territory of what is now Uruguay, on Brazil's southern borders, and Rio was a convenient centre from which to keep the danger under surveillance. The growing importance of the city was formally acknowledged in 1763 when Rio replaced Bahia as the capital of Brazil. The rule of the governors came to an end and was superseded by the rule of the viceroys. Through the viceroy the Crown kept a tight control over the city's government and trade. Wary of foreign influence, Lisbon saw to it that the new capital remained closed to the world's trade and the world's ideas.

The biggest single factor in opening up Rio was Napoleon. French forces, marching upon Lisbon under Marshal Junot at the height of the Peninsular War in November, 1807, caused the Prince Regent of Portugal (the future King João VI) and 10,000 of his courtiers to flee to their South American colony. Embarking at the eleventh hour in the ships of the Portuguese fleet, the royal court set sail for Brazil under the protection of British warships. They arrived in Rio in March, 1808, receiving a tumultuous welcome. The Prince Regent assumed direct rule in place of the viceroy, and the colonial capital became a royal capital.

Although the Regent was a soft and somewhat slovenly man (his fingers, it was said, were always sticky with chicken gravy) he nevertheless revolutionized the city and the lives of its inhabitants. Dom João's first act was to open the city to trade with friendly nations after nearly three centuries of Portuguese monopoly. The port experienced unprecedented activity. In 1808 only 90 foreign ships had entered Guanabara Bay; by 1822 the number had risen to 422.

In love with Brazil, Dom João declined to return to Portugal after Napoleon's final defeat in 1815. Instead, he proclaimed Brazil to be the equal of the mother country as a part of "The United Kingdom of Portugal, Brazil and the Algarves, of this side and the far side of the sea, the Guinea coast of Africa, and the conquest, navigation and commerce

The Long Rise out of Isolation

1500	Admiral Pedro Alvares Cabral discovers Brazil and claims it for Portugal
1502	Portuguese navigator André Gonçalves sails into Guanabara Bay on New Year's Day; mistaking it for an estuary, he names it Rio de Janeiro (River of January)
1503	Gonçalo Coelho, leader of a Portuguese exploration force, erects the first European-style stone building. Local Tamoio Indians call it the Carioca (House of the White Man)
1533	First sugar mill in Brazil built near present-day Santos, south-west of Rio
1538	First shipment of slaves from West Africa arrives in Brazil to work sugar plantations
1549	Portuguese colonial government formally established in Brazil by appointment of a Governor-General; Bahia made capital
1555	French Admiral Nicolas Durand de Villegaignon sets up fortress colony in Guanabara Bay as part of grand design to create a colonial empire called Antarctic France in southern Brazil
1560	Mem de Sá, Governor-General of Brazil, destroys the French fort but fails to oust the colonists from Guanabara Bay
1565	Estácio de Sá, Mem's nephew, founds a Portuguese settlement beneath Sugar Loaf and names it São Sebastião do Rio de Janeiro (Rio's official name), in honour of Portugal's King Sebastião
1567	Estácio and Mem de Sá rout the remaining French. Estácio is killed in battle
1570	São Sebastião settlement is moved northwards to Morro do Castelo, centre of the modern city. The first streets and square are built. First sugar mill in Rio established on Ilha do Governador
1600	City's population numbers 750 whites, 3,000 Indians and people of mixed race, and a hundred black slaves
1633	Benedictine Monastery of São Bento built in central district of Rio
1695	Gold discovered in Minas Gerais, inland from Rio; Guanabara Bay becomes main port for shipments of gold to Portugal
1703	Portugal enters War of Spanish Succession against France
1710	French force under Jean-François Du Clerc invades Rio but is defeated
1711	Rio sacked by French corsair René Duguay-Trouin. Ransom of gold, sugar and cattle exacted from its citizens in return for evacuation of city
1727	Jesuits introduce coffee into Brazil
1750	Carioca Aqueduct (Arcos da Carioca) completed, bringing water to city centre
1763	Rio succeeds Bahia as vice-regal capital of Brazil
1770	First coffee seedlings planted in Rio
1808	Prince Regent Dom João and 10,000 members of Portuguese court arrive in Rio after fleeing from Napoleon's army. City becomes de facto capital of Portuguese empire, and the port is opened to foreign shipping. Botanical Gardens founded
1810	Commercial treaty with Great Britain signed.
1815	Prince Regent declares Brazil and Portugal a united kingdom
1816	Dom João becomes King João VI of Brazil and Portugal. Mission of artists and scientists arrives in city from France
1821	João VI returns to Portugal, leaving his son Pedro as Prince Regent
1822	Brazil declared independent. Prince Regent crowned in Rio as Emperor Pedro I of Brazil
1830	Slave trade made illegal but enforcement of law ineffectual. Population of Rio estimated at 125,000

1831	Pedro I abdicates and returns to Lisbon, leaving his five-year-old son Pedro in Rio under a guardian. Brazil governed by regency
1840	Pedro, declared of age although only 14 years old, ascends throne as Emperor Pedro II
1850	Direct steamship service begun between Rio and Europe. New law suppresses slave trade
1854	Gaslights installed in city's streets
1857	Allan Kardec's "The Book of Spirits" published in Paris; later becomes basis of Brazilian spiritist movement called Kardecism
1858	First section of Dom Pedro II Railway opened, initiating growth of Rio's northern suburbs
1872	Population of Rio is 275,000
1877	Rio linked by rail to São Paulo
1888	Slavery abolished by act known as the Golden Law
1889	Brazil declared a Republic. Pedro II goes into exile after 49-year reign
1890	Public telephone service introduced in city
1892	Old Copacabana Tunnel built, linking Botafogo with Copacabana district
1897	Brazilian Academy of Letters founded
02-06	City undergoes major improvement and rebuilding. Health campaign eliminates yellow fever
1904	New Copacabana Tunnel built to accommodate increasing traffic. Avenidas Atlântica and Rio Branco laid out
1906	Rio Football League founded. Electric street lights introduced
1909	Municipal Theatre opened
1920	University of Rio de Janeiro founded. City's population exceeds one million
1922	Attempted military coup by officers of Copacabana Fort put down by loyal government forces. Morro do Castelo flattened and open space used for Brazilian Centenary Exhibition, which celebrates 100 years of independence
1928	First Carnival Samba School set up
1930	Government overthrown in military revolution. Getúlio Vargas, Governor of Rio Grande do Sul, becomes chief of provisional government
1931	Statue of Christ the Redeemer erected on Corcovado; paid for by subscription from Rio's churches
1937	Vargas suspends basic freedoms and makes himself dictator of Brazil
1938	Santos Dumont Airport completed on portion of Guanabara Bay shore extended with earth from Morro do Castelo
1941	First Congress of Spiritist Federation of Umbanda held
1942	Brazil enters Second World War on side of Allies
1943	Ministry of Education and Health building erected utilizing revolutionary reinforced-concrete design by Brazilian architects Oscar Niemeyer, Lúcio Costa and others
1945	Vargas deposed by military leaders; democratic government re-established
1950	Vargas becomes President in free elections. Maracanã Stadium, seating 200,000, built for World Cup soccer competition
1954	Vargas is deposed by military coup and commits suicide in presidential palace, Democratic institutions survive
1958	Museum of Modern Art, designed by Affonso Reidy, built
1960	Rio loses its position as Brazil's capital to new city of Brasília. Population of Rio reaches 3,307,000
1964	Military dictatorship established. João Goulart, President since 1961, flees Brazil
1968	Rebouças Tunnel links Lagoa district with North Zone of city
1974	Rio-Niterói bridge across Guanabara Bay opened. Population of city exceeds five million
1975	States of Guanabara and Rio de Janeiro merge. Rio becomes capital of newly enlarged State of Rio de Janeiro

to Ethiopia, Arabia, Persia and the Indies". It was the greatest colonial empire in the world at that time, and Rio de Janeiro—by now a city of 100,000—was its capital.

Yet Rio, early in Dom João's reign, was still provincial to the point of eccentricity, a hundred years behind Europe in urban amenities. The streets were unpaved and without public transport, illuminated at night only by the moon or a few whale-oil lamps, and infested by ruffians of all sorts. Dom João began to change all that. Rio was modernized, aired, improved, made to feel proud. The streets were paved, lighted and policed. The city acquired a new prosperity based on coffee, which was quickly becoming the main plantation crop. The necessities of civilized life began to appear. Most of the ships now entering Guanabara Bay were British, laden with the products of the early Industrial Revolution and bringing traders eager to exploit a virgin market. The British set up shop in Rio in a big way. Their emporiums were an Aladdin's Cave to the Cariocas, full of treasures they had never set eyes on or even dreamed of before: alarm clocks and false teeth; mouth organs and ice skates (which rusted unused); iron and porcelain and textile products of all kinds. The British changed the lifestyle of the Cariocas, gave them a taste for tea, ices, beer and bread, for cleaner streets and more sanitary houses and for the use of cutlery at meals (most Cariocas formerly ate with their hands and used a sheath knife to cut up meat).

While the influence of the British reflected their preoccupation with the material things of life, the influence of the French, who swarmed into Rio as refugees after the fall of Napoleon, reflected an intense involvement in life's pleasures. The French established themselves as confectioners, wine merchants, milliners, dressmakers, jewellers, hairdressers, tobacconists, perfumiers, and booksellers. They opened Rio's first hotel, the Pharoux, and gave Cariocas their first taste of French *haute cuisine*. After three centuries of African and indigenous tropical influences—in food, domestic architecture, living habits—the colonists of Rio began to be re-Europeanized, adopting even the clothing of the carboniferous civilization of the Old World—drab frock coats, boots and top hats quite unsuited to the steaming tropic world of Guanabara.

The Cariocas also began to enjoy the kind of civilized institutions that had previously been banned because of their insurrectionary potential. The Regent founded the city's first printers, the first newspaper, the first library; he founded the first military and naval academies in the country, the first bank (the Bank of Brazil), the first medical school and the first theatre and museum; he founded an observatory and an academy of fine arts, staffed by French academicians.

Imbued with the ideals of the Romantic movement, Dom João tried to impart to the Cariocas his love of the primeval natural surroundings of the city. The Cariocas had always cringed from the wilderness, viewing it as a disadvantage to be overcome. But the Regent made a virtue of it. He chose as his royal residence an inaccessible out-of-town place called Quinta da Boa Vista, bequeathed to him by one of the richest merchants of Rio. He built numerous villas in the remoter parts of the countryside and on uninhabited little jungle islands in the bay. He opened new paths through the Tijuca forest, and founded Rio's Botanical Gardens. There he planted the first imperial palm, from which all the imperial palms that embellish the city today are descended. He introduced the habit of sea bathing (little did he guess to how far later Cariocas would carry that salubrious fad). His son rode all over the countryside and climbed to the top of Corcovado, the first white man to do so.

At the invitation of Dom João, scientists and artists poured into the city. From Austria came a mission that included the naturalists Johann Baptist Spix and Carl Friedrich Philipp von Martius, and the landscape painter Thomas Ender. A French mission brought the architect Victor Grandjean de Montigny and the artist Jean-Baptiste Debret. More were to follow in the years to come—men like the great naturalist Louis Agassiz, the naturalist Charles Darwin, the explorer and scholar Sir Richard Burton. These eminent visitors produced books and pictures that give an exceptionally full and vivid account of Brazil and the Rio society of those days— still colonial, patriarchal and slave-based, but swiftly becoming more integrated with the rest of the world.

In their drawings and paintings of that exotic city so long closed to prying eyes, the lie of the land is the same as today: the drooping palms and lianas, the broad sweep of the bay before the city, Sugar Loaf on the skyline, Corcovado (without its statue) dominating the city. Some of Thomas Ender's beautiful views—the hospital of Misericórdia, Glória Church on its hill, and the thoroughfare of the Rua Direita (later Rua 1° de Março)—look much as they do now, a century and a half later. But the pictures of that time portray human figures so exotic and so extraordinary that it is difficult to believe they ever existed. In the streets there are soldiers wearing high-plumed helmets and gay, blue Hussars' uniforms; goat-bearded merchants in sombreros and cloaks, frock-coated tax collectors carrying leather-bound ledgers and gold-tipped canes, Chinese coolies brought in to experiment with tea-planting in the royal Botanical Gardens, men on horseback, black girls with buckets on their heads, and people slumped in the shade of doorways, trees, and awnings.

These scenes admirably convey the authentic look of things in Rio then, the brilliant colours of the place, the luxuriance of the vegetation. They do not convey the heat and the sweat, the hubbub of the markets and quayside, the cries of the black street vendors, the boom of the fortress guns signalling the opening and closing of the bay at 5 a.m. and 10 p.m., the stink of the beaches where the slaves daily emptied barrels of domestic ordure so that it could be washed away by the tide.

A courtyard in a surviving pocket of 18th-Century Rio retains decorative flourishes typical of the era, including a baroque fountain with swan's-neck spout and blue-patterned Portuguese tiles known as azulejos.

In Rio, travellers were indeed ravished by the beauty of the exterior world, by its views and natural history, but they were repelled by the interior world, by the dark, airless houses smelling of chamber pots and by the patriarchal lifestyle that dominated them. The man of the house was a total autocrat, with the power of life and death over even his own sons. He presided over meals, seated in a large chair resembling a throne, and he kept the womenfolk in a state of subjection resembling Mohammedan purdah. The women were allowed into the streets only behind the heavy drapes of a sedan chair, and if they attended church on a feast day their faces generally had to be veiled. They were not permitted to be seen by male visitors to the house. They received next to no education, talked to almost no one but their slave girls and pet monkeys, and had practically nothing to do but eat jellies, smoke cigars and read. Fat, pale and sickly, they lived out their days behind thick walls and closed shutters, barely stirring from their divans or hammocks, overwhelmed by a lifetime's ennui and fatuity. At 12 or 13 they were married off to husbands of 50 or 60, and if they were still single at the age of 15, they were thought to be almost on the shelf. They were released from their boredom only by the occasional catharsis of the church confessional or perhaps by a premature death as they gave birth to a tenth child at the age of 25. Their husbands paid them little attention, reserving their ardour for the intimate embrace of young women of African descent or the exciting demi-mondaines of the cafés.

More shocking to the Europeans was the prevalence of slaves. Everywhere the visitors looked, they saw slaves in loincloths, slaves in braided jackets, slaves in chains, slaves labouring not only as stevedores and navvies but as valets to their perspiring masters, helping them off with their hats, mopping their brows, handing them their food and drink. In Rio everyone had slaves, even the beggars who sought alms from hammocks carried by slaves. In a city which boasted not a single steam engine or mechanically driven machine, slaves were the human power plants, the basis of industry. They constituted two-thirds of the population of 60,000 in 1808, and this proportion remained constant over the next 10 years, when the population doubled. To meet the labour demands of the booming coffee plantations, the number of slaves coming in from Africa was higher than ever. Between 1820 and 1829, a total of 256,000 were brought in, and 53,000 in 1829 alone. By this time the humanitarian crusade against slavery was gaining impetus in Europe, but in isolated Brazil the institutions of slavery and the slave trade were still for the most part blandly accepted.

Dom João ruled Brazil as Prince Regent for eight years. In 1816, his mother, old and mad, died in Portugal. Now King João VI, he was subjected to increasing pressure to return to Portugal, and in 1821 he was obliged to sail for Lisbon, leaving his son Pedro as Regent in Brazil. Blundering Portuguese attempts to reduce Brazil again to dependent status so alienated the colony that nationalist and separatist feeling began to burn high. Pedro was forced to choose between heading the independence movement or losing control of Brazil. He summoned a constituent assembly in Rio and on September 7, 1822, dramatically proclaimed Brazilian independence, putting himself at the country's head as Emperor Pedro I. This manoeuvre allowed Brazil to achieve its freedom without the trauma that shook most of the Spanish colonies in Latin America, which were forced to wage war for their independence. But the Emperor, after a promising start, proceeded to rule as a despotic monarch, and after nine years of waning popularity he was forced to abdicate in 1831. In 1840, after a decade of regency, his eldest son attained his majority at the age of 14 and was crowned Emperor of Brazil as Dom Pedro II.

The young Emperor was a Bourbon on his father's side, a Braganza on his mother's side, and also a Habsburg on his mother's side. His prognathous Habsburg jaw was hidden by a bushy beard, but in profile he looked like a cashew nut. Although he was authoritarian with his cabinet ministers, his rule was timid and liberal, and he was affectionately regarded by the people, who called him Pedro Banana (a play on the word Braganza) and forgave him his illicit love affairs because he had such an ugly wife.

The Emperor was very interested in scientific developments. He was the first man in Brazil to have his photograph taken and the first to speak on a telephone. During his 49-year reign, Rio lost the last of its colonial flavour and became a recognizable modern metropolis. The sedan chairs and palanquins disappeared from the streets and were replaced by street-cars called *bondes*, which ran on rails and were pulled by mules. The streets echoed with the clop of hoofs and the rattle of carriages—cabs, tilburies, victorias, coupés, landaus—and, after 1858, with the hooting and hissing of the steam locomotives rumbling down the first stretch of the Dom Pedro II Railway to Queimados. The railway helped to push the suburbs out farther and farther to north and west, until the tentacles of the city reached round the back of the mountains that had hitherto limited the spread of settlement. The first sewage disposal system was initiated in 1864, and in 1874 Dom Pedro himself went down to the desert beach of Copacabana to inaugurate a submarine telegraph cable between Rio and London.

By now the slave trade was a thing of the past. It had been declared illegal in 1830, but continued illegally and even expanded until the 1850s, when the British took matters into their own hands and sent naval squadrons to the west coast of Africa and into Brazilian territorial waters and ports to suppress it. The Africanization of Brazil was over: with no further blacks arriving, with immigration from Portugal, Italy and Spain rising, the population entered a period of gradual "bleaching" which has continued to the present day.

There was still no law against the ownership of slaves in Brazil, however, and by the 1880s emancipation had become the chief political

In a hilly suburb, a decaying 18th-Century house faces inwards on its own courtyard, recalling the cloistered lives led by the middle and upper classes in colonial Rio. Women were rarely allowed out, except when going to visit the houses of their friends.

issue of the day. Many Brazilians were ashamed that theirs was the only Christian nation that still condoned slavery, and although the coffee planters and great landowners resisted abolition, popular feeling was too strong for them. In 1888 the Brazilian parliament passed the so-called Golden Law, freeing all slaves. Princess Isabel, a committed abolitionist, signed it while her father, the Emperor, was absent abroad. Twenty-five years had passed since slavery had been abolished in the United States and 55 years since it had been abolished in the British colonies.

The monarchy was a casualty of these changes. "You have redeemed a race but lost a crown," the Princess was told by anti-abolitionists when she signed the Golden Law. Conservative landowners were so alienated by the uncompensated expropriation of their slaves that they would not support the royal family against the growing republicanism of the army and the new urban middle class. On November 15, 1889, the royal family was summarily banished from Brazil, and the country was declared a republic. The Emperor, outliving his wife by a few months, died forlorn in a second-rate hotel in Paris two years later.

Rio had proceeded from pioneering outpost to vice-regal seat to royal capital to republican capital—and now the modern era of rapid population growth and comprehensive urban redevelopment was about to begin. Already, aided by massive immigration from Europe and the beginnings of immigration from the Brazilian countryside, the population was touching half a million. The old Rio would soon disappear, but not the memory of its earlier ages. For me, perhaps, the Golden Age was the age of Debret and Thomas Ender, when hyacinth macaws still screamed in the forest, the bay was full of sails and the city lay squashed like a mango around the foot of its hills, when every step was a new discovery and Brazil's ruler preferred his tropical colony to his European homeland.

To forge a personal link with those brilliant and distant days in Rio, I paid a visit to the royal family's old summer palace at Petrópolis. There I called on the present incumbent—the pretender to the throne of Brazil, Dom Pedro Gastão, Prince of Orléans and Braganza. He is descended in a direct line from João VI, Pedro I and Pedro II. He is the grandson of Princess Isabel, who signed the abolition of slavery, and he would have succeeded to the throne if the monarchy had continued.

Petrópolis is a small hill town to the north of Rio, 2,000 feet up in the beautiful Organ Mountains at the landward end of Guanabara Bay. Cool and green and peaceful, it is a favourite place for people who do not care for the noisy crowds and the heat of the big city. The second Emperor had been one of those people. He spent a lot of time in the Grão-Pará Palace (now the Imperial Museum), and his descendant Prince Pedro still lives in an annex of the palace—a long, elegant, terracotta building with many shuttered windows and a double front door. I knocked on the door.

Brazilian naval ships in Guanabara Bay dock by a Ministry of Marine building, a Gothic fantasy built as a customs house in the 1880s by Emperor Pedro II.

It was opened by Dom Pedro Gastão João Maria Philipe Lorenço Humberto Miguel Rafael Gonzago de Orléans e Bragança himself. Formally he was addressed as "Your Highness", informally as Pedrinho, little Peter. He was tall, upright, almost military looking, somewhat Germanic (his mother was an Austrian countess), with grey hair and a grey moustache. His gold teeth gleamed when he smiled.

"Good day!" he exclaimed cheerily in curious schoolboy English. "How do you do? Happy to meet you. Please." Those were the last words of English he spoke; for the rest of the afternoon he conversed with me in Portuguese or French.

I went into the palace annex. There were halberds on the wall. In the large ante-room hung portraits of João VI, Pedro I and Pedro II. There was a little girl in the fireplace, about two years old. She was crying.

"Excuse me," His Highness said, "she's got stuck in the chimney." The little girl had her head up the chimney and her legs entangled in the fire dogs. He extracted the child and beckoned me on to a long colonnaded verandah full of potted plants and easy chairs. A handsome young woman was drinking coffee. She was Princess Maria Joana, one of his daughters and the mother of the child.

"My daughter is called Maria," said the Prince, "and my wife is called Maria, and the little girl, she is called Maria, and I have another daughter, who is married to Prince Alexander of Yugoslavia, and she is called Maria. This is due entirely to lack of imagination."

I was given coffee. The cups bore the imperial coat of arms of the last Emperor of Brazil, a laurel garland enclosing the monogram P followed by the Roman numeral II and surmounted by a crown.

"I am sorry my wife is not here," said the Prince. "She is the aunt of King Juan Carlos of Spain. I have a sister who is the Countess of Paris— she would be the next queen of France. As for me, yes, I am head of the royal family of Brazil, but I wouldn't call that my job exactly. Actually I run a real estate company in Petrópolis, one that Dom Pedro II used to own."

He told me that he was born in France in 1913, when the royal family was still under order of banishment from Brazil. In 1922, on the 100th anniversary of Independence, this order was revoked, and when Dom Pedro was 11 years old he returned with his family to the homeland he had never seen. "Although I was born a Frenchman," His Highness explained, "our family had always been instilled with a passion for Brazil, for its soil, its flowers, its fruit, everything."

Dom Pedro was an ardent conservationist and a pioneer campaigner against pollution. We went into the garden. To one side rose hills covered in luxurious tropical forest. The trees, bedecked with brilliant yellow and mauve blossoms, were part of the old imperial estate and some of them were more than a hundred years old. Some property developers and timber merchants wanted to cut these down, but the Prince had refused to let them do so. Their beauty was the inheritance of Petrópolis, he said, and ought to be shared by all.

Many birdcages hung from stands in the garden, and the air was full of the cry of parrots and bell birds and Amazon jacamins. The Prince took a black starling-like bird, a graúna, out of its cage. It perched on his head, then flew off. "Come back, you little rascal!" cried His Highness, running after it behind a hedge. In a little while he came back clutching the bird. He put it back in the cage, talking to it and whistling and cooing.

"Little rascal," he said, and to me, "I expect you would like to have a look round now." The annex where he lived with his family had been the quarters of courtiers in the royalist days. It seemed to be furnished almost entirely with the possessions of his forebears—a museum brought to life by the family atmosphere pervading it. There was French paper on the walls, and there were fine cedar doors, books and ceramics and silver and pictures and mementoes of all sorts. "This is a travelling whisky glass Queen Victoria gave my great-grandfather," said the Prince. "Don't drop it."

I told him that Queen Victoria drank a lot of whisky, half a bottle in the morning. "That's why she had the whisky glass handy," said the Prince. "I can't think why else she gave it."

In the dining-room, a magnificent moth with six-inch wings fluttered among the cutlery and silver candlesticks on a long, shiny table. The Prince tried to catch it, but it took refuge high up on the window drapes, its wings outstretched like a patch of faded tapestry. We went into the study, and the Prince rummaged in a cupboard and produced a big brown minute book, every page full of graceful writing.

"The second Emperor of Brazil's unpublished memoirs," said His Highness. "Or, more exactly, his thoughts about life. He was very fond of literature and always corresponding with famous writers: Victor Hugo, people like that. But he was not a very good writer himself. In fact, he was a rotten writer."

We went to the Prince's bedroom. There was an old four-poster by the fireside, with a wooden cradle at the foot of it. A very lovely princess with blonde hair and pale blue eyes and the body of an athlete was rummaging through the drawers of a dressing-table. She was wearing jeans and an American football shirt with the number 88 on it.

"This is Cristina," her father explained. "She has just come back from the Amazon."

"What part of the Amazon?" I asked her.

"Amapá," she said. "The Serra do Navio."

"I know the Serra do Navio," I said. It is a low mountain range covered in rain forests inland from the north bank of the Lower Amazon, thronged with mosquitoes and alligators. I was full of admiration.

"I discovered a hummingbird unknown to science there," she added. "It was named after me. Tremetes Cristinae."

What a splendid family, I thought. Had the last Emperor's family been like this? If so, how could Brazilians have wanted to get rid of them?

The Prince suggested we take a look at the palace proper. "Get the dog in and shut the door behind you, will you," His Highness said. I closed the door on the dog, the golden crown on a chair, the halberds on the wall.

A black street cleaner was sweeping the gutter outside. "Hello," His Highness said to him, shaking the road sweeper's hand. "How is your wife?"

The bells of the grey cathedral where the remains of Dom Pedro II are now entombed were pealing over the elegant houses of the quiet hill town. The palace was on the other side of a grassy square shaded with trees. It was closed for redecoration but the Prince insisted on showing me around.

"This is my great-grandfather's crown," he said. "Solid gold, with 639 diamonds and 77 pearls. It weighs 1,720 grammes. It was made in Rio for the Emperor's coronation in 1841. And this is his sceptre; and this is the Order of the Garter that Queen Victoria gave him; and this . . ." We looked down at the table on which his grandmother had signed the order liberating millions of Brazilians from slavery.

"All these things actually belong to me," said the Prince. "But of course, I have lent them to the museum on a permanent basis. As head of the Brazilian royal family, I am naturally a monarchist. But if ever the monarchy was restored and I had to be made King of Brazil, I could only say *que horrível abacaxi!* What a hash-up!"

With this quintessentially Cariocan quip he let me out. As I crossed the grassy square and drove away from Petrópolis, I thought: "What a very nice pretender to the throne His Highness was; how modest and good humoured." He was a popular figure in Petrópolis, and he rode around the streets on his horse, sometimes accompanied by a goat cart for the children. If ever there had to be another monarch of Brazil, I thought, the Brazilians would be very lucky with this one.

Scenes from a Slave Society

Out for a stroll, a Rio civil servant observes old-fashioned Portuguese custom by leading his family in single file, while slaves follow in order of rank.

When the royal court of Portugal moved to its colony of Brazil in 1808 to escape Napoleon's invading armies, Rio—hitherto a jealously guarded preserve—was thrown open to foreigners for the first time. Visitors were welcomed into the city, and among them came the painter Jean-Baptiste Debret, who arrived in 1816 as a member of a French cultural mission. Reproduced here are some of the impressions of Rio he published after his return to Paris in the 1830s. The life style reflected in his studies was a curious amalgam of out-dated Portuguese manners and tropical indolence. But above all, as Debret's careful drawings and thorough commentary make plain, it was a society in which every facet of life depended on the labour and skills of an army of black slaves—still being imported from Africa at the rate of tens of thousands each year.

As their easy-going guard chats with a woman, chained slaves, convicted of such crimes as theft or absconding, pause during a water-carrying detail to buy tobacco at a street-side stall. Even while serving penal terms, slaves could often contrive to raise a little money, either by selling small items of their own handiwork or by begging from passers-by.

New arrivals from Africa await their fate in a slave dealer's establishment while the seated proprietor negotiates the sale of a child to an up-country customer. Almost half the slaves shipped to Brazil died within five years, usually from disease or overwork.

Among the activities of an early morning in Rio, a pious old woman (foreground) pays a coin for the privilege of kissing a holy image, slaves bring fresh water for the day and lower a whale-oil street lamp for refilling (left), and an officer employed to raise money for a religious fraternity uses his upturned umbrella to catch a contribution (right).

The quayside in late afternoon is populated by white citizens savouring a quiet chat with friends and the offerings of sweet-sellers. Even whites of modest means usually owned two or three slaves, whose labours enabled them to lead a comfortable and leisurely life.

Watched by his half-breed wife, a Portuguese cobbler (above) punishes a slave with a special instrument called a palmatoria; holes in its business end lessened air resistance as it was swung, permitting a more painful blow. A slave had no appeal from whatever form of discipline his master chose to inflict.

Two young slaves ply their skills as street barbers in Rio's main square. Such work was done without supervision, but they had to report twice a day to their masters to hand in their earnings. In this scene, the customers—although also slaves—are obviously men of standing: the medallion worn by one indicates his employment in the customs service.

Dining at home with her taciturn husband, a Rio matron treats the babies of slaves to titbits from the table. When black children reached the age of five or six, such indulgence ceased and they were banished to the slaves' quarters to learn the realities of life.

Three trusted slave couples in a rich household are married in a joint ceremony. Formal unions among the slaves of a single house were often encouraged by the owner as a means of promoting loyalty—and also because the offspring resulting from the marriages provided him with new slaves at no cost.

Held on the lap of its black nurse, a new-born white child is carried in a litter to church for baptism. For this important occasion, a nurse was usually caparisoned in all the finest clothes and jewels the family could muster.

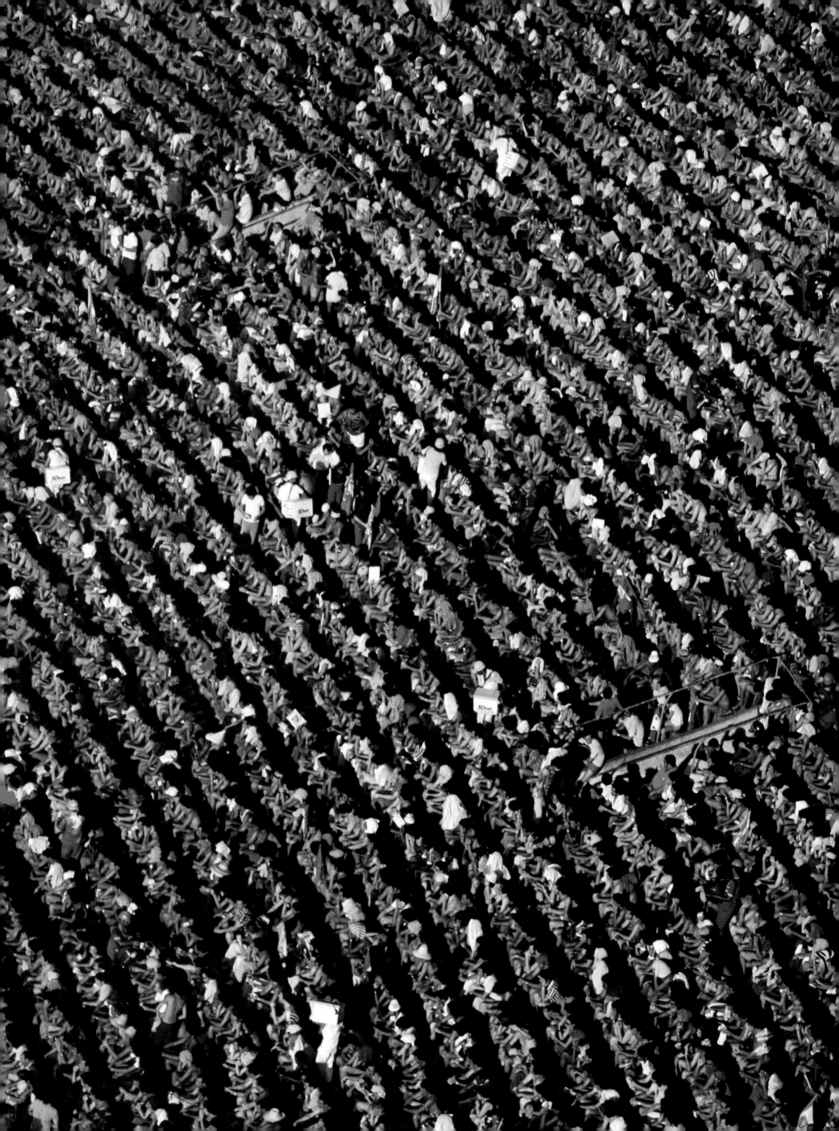

4

Joe Carioca

When Walt Disney Productions decided to send Donald Duck to South America for the 1943 film *Saludos Amigos*, the scriptwriters devised a cigar-chewing green parrot to be his Brazilian guide, mentor and friend. The bird was rumbustious and talkative, flew upside down, and was given to squawking and acting crazily. They called it Joe Carioca. It was a grotesque caricature of the average inhabitant of Rio, but the people it lampooned weren't offended. Self-mockery is something of a Rio tradition, and most Cariocas laughed at their embodiment as a cartoon parrot.

The Carioca, in fact, generally resorts to broad stereotypes if asked to define himself, and he accepts quite naturally the notion that the people of Rio are somehow different from everybody else. The Carioca, he will tell you, is intensely gregarious. Like his Disney namesake he talks fast and incessantly; his conversation is brilliant, larded with irreverent wisecracks and soaring flights of fancy—and often meaningless. He is sophisticated, individualistic, easy-going and above all pleasure-loving.

This mass portrait is recognized throughout Brazil. Even by his fellow-countrymen the Carioca is considered extraordinary. In the interior he stands out as a foreigner. The people of São Paulo see the Carioca as lazy, unambitious and unreliable; the Amazonians see him as outrageous in speech and behaviour. The Carioca, on the other hand, views the Paulista as a neurotic materialist and the Amazonian as a country bumpkin.

It is surprising that there should be so much unanimity about the Carioca personality, given the differences that exist between classes and racial groups in Rio. If there is a common personality underlying all the economic and social diversity, it can have its roots only in something in the city itself. Much of it must grow from the languorous tropical environment that has given the city its atmosphere of sensual hedonism and indolence. The Austrian-born writer Stefan Zweig noted that "there is something soft and relaxing in the air, making humanity less aggressive—and possibly less energetic". Rich and poor alike also share the city's other mood, the noise and bustle that dominates the streets. Cariocas of every class thrive on crowds, the pulse of the samba, the restless *movimento* and late nights of the city. ("The Carioca night," the saying goes, "has more than twelve hours.")

To understand this constant, untiring need for activity, it is necessary to remember that the Carioca has often *chosen* an urban life. The immigrants who flow by the tens of thousands into Rio are prompted to do so not merely by the hardships of rural Brazilian life, but also by an

Rank upon rank of soccer fans, most of them shirtless in the afternoon sun, fill Rio's Maracanã Stadium, a vast concrete arena that can hold 200,000 spectators. Football fever runs so high that the playing field is surrounded by a nine-foot-deep moat that serves to keep the excited spectators at bay.

eagerness to sample the diversions of the metropolis. This is even more true of the up-country entrepreneurs who leave big estates in the interior to settle among the fleshpots of Copacabana. Few of these new urbanites look back on the land they came from with anything other than distaste.

Cariocas in general have little feeling for nature and the countryside. Not for them the back-to-the-land values of Wordsworth and Thoreau. By settling for life in a teeming hillside slum or crowded apartment block, by losing themselves on a packed beach or in an overflowing football stadium, by turning their radios up to full volume, they shut out that vast and terrible Brazilian wilderness where the jaguars growl and the ants bite and every stranger carries a gun; they defy the silence out there, the loneliness, the boredom that descends at nightfall. The Carioca is a man of the streets; he is only truly happy with solid asphalt beneath his feet, or that form of hexagonal paving-stone he calls quaintly *paralelepípedo*.

If an Englishman's home is his castle, a Carioca's is his bivouac, a base from which he sallies forth to forage and dally and carouse with his boon companions and to which he returns to snatch sleep and sustenance. For the Carioca there are no escapist day-dreams, no secret longings for enchanted places. He is in one already. Rio, he will never cease to remind himself, is the *Cidade Maravilhosa*, the enchanted city, and Copacabana is the most beautiful beach in the world. Even the most sophisticated and well travelled Carioca believes this, and to a large extent he is right.

I once asked a Carioca friend what he thought of Petrópolis, the hill town up in the Organ Mountains, whose air and landscape I, as a North European, found congenial. His answer was illuminating.

"Petrópolis is the second most boring place I have ever been in," he said. "It is dull and old and provincial. It has no *movimento*. The climate is cold and wretched. The countryside is ugly, all boring forests and mountains and things. And there is nothing to do at night. I would hate to live there."

"If Petrópolis is the second most boring place," I asked my friend, "what is the most boring place of all?"

"Africa," he replied. "All of it. There is nothing whatsoever to see in Africa. And Kenya is the worst of all. Like a huge Petrópolis with millions of dangerous animals roaming all over it."

I had never come across such an absolutely urban outlook before. I spent several years of my life in Kenya and to me it has always been the most exhilarating place in the world. But then, I am not a Carioca.

"So what is the most beautiful place you have ever seen?" I asked my friend. Without hesitation he answered, "Copacabana in the early morning when the sun is streaming into the streets and the newspaper kiosks are just opening and the traffic is just beginning to flow down the Avenida Atlântica and radios are playing in the windows and people are starting to go down to the beach. Then it is the most beautiful place in the world."

In the early hours of the afternoon, when customers are few and far between, a soft-drinks and ice-cream vendor takes time off to rest on his stall. Rio's many street stands sell such Brazilian specialities as guaraná, a juice made from an Amazonian fruit, as well as locally bottled American colas.

For all its charms, Rio suffers grievous problems—overcrowding, traffic congestion, pollution—from having grown according to the dictates of no higher logic than that of expediency. The Carioca's solution to living in such chaos is to adopt a philosophy of pragmatic individualism. He is not a group man, and everyday life in Rio is not a harmonious co-existence but a permanent muddle in which everyone fends for himself. The Carioca is tacitly and implicitly against authority, against the state, against taxes, against the rule of law and the rule of rules. The notion of every man for himself lies at the heart of Cariocan civics.

Cariocas will often describe themselves by referring to two closely related figures of the city's folklore, the *moleque* and the *malandro*. The *moleque* is a street arab, an artful dodger who treats even the most serious matters in the lightest possible way. The *malandro* is a master of opportunism and improvisation; he lives by his wits and always tries to get something for nothing. Fable pictures him as residing in a favela, where he leads a life of continual adventure and raises hell for the fun of it, a guitar in one hand, a razor blade in the other.

There is a bit of the *moleque* and the *malandro* in every Carioca. The *moleque* in him gives him the capacity to take life as it comes and enjoy its pleasures. Whatever the actual zodiacal sign of his birth, the chances are that he will be typically Piscean in character. His thought processes are imaginative rather than intellectual, emotional rather than rational, mystical rather than practical.

"We are very brilliant," one Rio university lecturer explained to me, "and very superficial and oblique. We are not penetrating or powerful or profound. But we are graceful, witty, fluent and full of panache. We have never produced a Schopenhauer or a Sartre and I don't suppose we ever shall. We don't go in for what the Western world calls greatness of mind and thought. We are content with the surface of things, with how things look and sound and taste and feel and smell, rather than what they mean. A girl's bottom, if I may say so, is as significant to us as a theory of the universe. We appreciate a nice picture as we enjoy nice food; we taste it and admire it and ask no questions. We like a good tune, a good story, and a pretty poem. So we are strong in music, lyric poetry and narrative fiction, and in the plastic arts. And the same goes for pop culture generally. Rio gave the world samba and bossa nova and modern Carnival. All beat and mood and sex. The celebration of the body rather than of the mind. There is not so much wrong with that."

The *malandro* side of the Carioca makes him admire the fixer, the gambler, the man who takes chances. He is prepared to work hard when necessary, and in times of inflation he may even hold down two or three jobs at a time to make ends meet. But his heart does not lie in industriousness of this kind. He does not share the Paulista's work ethic. He is rarely punctual; and the excuses he concocts for his lateness or non-arrival are masterpieces of invention, often involving the alleged death of some distant relative. Work for him is a regrettable fact of life, made necessary by his even greater distaste for poverty.

The middle-class Carioca has inherited that indelible Brazilian tradition known as the gentleman complex, the attitude of the plantation owner of days gone by, to whom idle dignity and even dignified poverty always seemed better and nobler than an insane struggle for daily bread. Thus in the bigger firms in Rio de Janeiro, the top jobs often go to non-Cariocas, Brazilians with more drive and less hedonism than the native. As for the working-class Carioca, he chooses idleness whenever the comparison between effort expended and reward obtained appears unfavourable to him. In all classes of society, the Carioca tends to be more impressed by the quick buck than the honest penny. If he can succeed without actually trying, then so much the better.

One of the most popular ways of making easy money is gambling. The state-run Federal Lottery, established in 1961, now has an annual turnover equivalent to hundreds of millions of dollars a year. It proved so successful that a second government-operated sweepstake—this one a national football pool called the Sporting Lottery—was introduced in 1969; two years later, the pool paid out more than $2 million to a single winner, a world-record prize at the time.

The longest established Brazilian lottery is a clandestine racket called the *jogo do bicho*, or animal numbers game, which has been going for the better part of a century. Although it has been illegal since 1941, it has thrived under cover. It has remained the most honestly run illegal gambling game in the world, with winnings scrupulously paid out in full at 20 to 1 or 70 to 1 or even 5,000 to 1.

The game was invented in 1893 by the rich and reputable Baron de Drummond. The Baron owned a zoological garden that was open to the public (it later became the city zoo) and received municipal support for the maintenance of the animals. When the city council cut his grant, he decided to make up the money by introducing a game of chance for visitors to his zoo. The gamble was to guess which of 25 pictures of animals —ostrich, elephant, goat, butterfly, peacock, and so on—was the one the Baron had chosen the night before and placed in a sealed bag. The game caught on, and people flocked to his zoo.

Before long, the *jogo do bicho* captured the interest of underworld entrepreneurs all over the country. While retaining the basic features worked out by the Baron, these operators devised new and more complicated permutations: groups of numbers were provided for each animal, so that a gambler going for high stakes had to guess up to four numbers in their correct order. Such refinements helped the game attain the status of a major industry. By the mid-1970s, 30,000 people—controlled by a handful of enormously wealthy "bankers"—were reckoned to be em-

Earning his livelihood as a street showman, a fire-eater at the Fiera da Norte—a Sunday market in the northern suburb of São Cristovão —prepares to swallow two mouthfuls of flaming petrol as a mesmerized audience looks on.

ployed in running the game in Rio alone, and the daily turnover approached $1 million.

The Government has repeatedly attempted to stamp out this subterranean pastime, sometimes with dismaying results: during one crackdown on corruption, investigators discovered that half the city's policemen were receiving pay-offs from the game's operators. In the mid-1970s, the authorities, working on the "If you can't beat them, join them" principle, introduced their own version of the game, a third national sweepstake known as the Zooteca or Popular Lottery.

The Carioca's appetite for games of chance, however enormous, is nothing compared to his obsession with sex. Rio is a sexy city, though not a sin city. Sexual outlets of one kind or another are just as available—or just as inaccessible, depending on your point of view—as in any other large modern metropolis. Where Rio differs from some other cities is in making such a public virtue out of its sexiness. Cariocas, both male and female, tend to represent themselves as figures of heroic sexual prowess and allure. Some Cariocas probably are, although most—life being what it is— are probably not. Londoners do not go around extolling the attractions of London girls: pubs, yes, taxis, maybe, but not girls, nice as they are. Parisians do not, for the benefit of any stranger in earshot, go around declaiming: "Of course, we Parisians are fantastic in bed." In Rio they do all these things: it is the role they play.

How the sexual mystique of Rio arose is hard to explain. The family has always been the most fundamental institution in Rio society, and the virtue of its female members has always been considered sacrosanct. Until 20 years ago, you couldn't take a girl to the pictures without a chaperone. Rio is still more conservative than many other cities in North America and Europe. Its reputation as a centre of carnality seems to have been a Brazilian rather than a foreign invention, the product of the outraged sensibilities of straightlaced provincials from the interior, whose stricter Latin-American Catholic mores were offended by the relative libertinage of the big city.

The Carioca still has the power to shock in the remoter, more conservative towns of Brazil. I remember having dinner one night in a restaurant in Belém, the port at the mouth of the Amazon. The restaurant was called the Maloca, the Brazilian name for the Amazon Indian's communal hut, and it was built like one—a circular grass and wattle hut, lit by candles inside, and decorated with Indian spears, bows, headdresses, fetish masks, a stuffed boa constrictor coiled round a roof-beam, and a glass tank of piranhas searching the weeds for scraps of flesh. On a small, circular dance floor in the centre of the hut a number of couples danced to over-amplified music. Above the dancers' heads, a woman with a large spotlight stood on a small bamboo platform. She was there to enforce public decency on behalf of the restaurant proprietors. When two Cariocas began dancing in the uninhibitedly sensual style fashionable in Rio—mouth glued to mouth, pelvis to pelvis—the music suddenly stopped and the spotlight snapped on. It swung on to the offending couple, who were bluntly told to leave the restaurant.

The Calvinist tradition of guilt about the sins of the flesh is entirely alien to Carioca males. A boy is tacitly encouraged to embark on sexual adventures with women as soon as he is physically able or mentally inclined. By the time he is adult, he has (so he claims) the appetite of a stallion. This is all part of the deeply rooted ethic of machismo—an extreme form of assertively virile masculinity in a male-dominated society. A macho man is strong, bold, masterful and lusty; he is Priapus incarnate; he devours women for breakfast. The ideals of machismo, elsewhere in the world deemed old-fashioned, are dying slowly. When a pretty girl walks by it is still *de rigueur* for all Carioca males, irrespective of age or job or class, to follow her with an unblinking stare and ritually explore her body from head to foot, admiring her *malemoléncia*, her slow, soft, hip-swaying gait, in imitation of which—so some people say—the undulating pavement patterns of the Avenida Atlântica were created. When a man takes an interest in a woman in Rio, she is not under any illusions as to the reason. It is not her wit, it is not a need for a deep relationship, or for friendship or love or any other abstraction; it is her anatomy he is after, for in Rio *eros* is stronger than *caritas*.

In the world of machismo, the female is prey and victim. Ipanema is the predatory male's favourite hunting-ground: the Ipanema hanger-out—

Three Cariocas demonstrate the minimalist mode of attire that prevails in the streets of Ipanema: the two women above gossip with the owner of a motor cycle—a potent status symbol among the young and trendy—while on the left an older resident gets a foretaste of the sun on his way down to the beach.

usually young, rich, leisured, white and trendy—is the quintessential Carioca macho. He makes his pick-ups at crowded bar-restaurants on the pavement above the beach, often cruising slowly past in a car, alone or with friends, and jumping out to proposition any unescorted girls who may be sitting at the tables.

Often the chosen targets are mulatta girls. The attitude of young white males towards mulattas casts an interesting sidelight on racial relations in Rio. The words "mulatto" and "mulatta" are not disparaging terms; they are used by all classes in the city and simply mean brown. To the macho male, though, "mulatta" has an especially pleasant ring. It conjures up images of slinky sexuality that set the imagination racing. The mulatta is generally considered the symbol of sensuality, and it is accepted for white men in Rio to have brown-skinned girl friends. Yet the façade of racial equality presented by this easy sexual familiarity is deceptive. Such relationships rarely extend to marriage, and the lingering racism that haunts Brazilian sexual attitudes is summed up in an old saying that can still be heard in Rio: "A white woman is for marrying, a mulatta for making love, a black woman for working."

Although racial attitudes are slow to change, machismo generally is coming under attack. Feminine emancipation and Western permissiveness have changed the old hunter-hunted stereotype in the sexual affairs of the city. I was interested to see a reversal of the old order one evening when four girls in a car drove slowly past a restaurant, then stopped and propositioned a couple of astonished young men; when the men showed interest, the girls jeered, put their thumbs to their noses and drove off.

The Carioca girl is no longer backward in coming forward. In part this reflects the change in emphasis on female virginity. In an opinion poll taken in Rio during the 1960s, 83 per cent of the male respondents insisted that a woman should be a virgin before she got married. That figure was halved in a recent poll. But men in Rio still tend to view women as their personal property after marriage and expect them to be totally faithful to them, without feeling bound to be faithful in return: 71 per cent of the Cariocas sampled in the recent poll expected a man to have extra-marital sex. This imposes a tremendous emotional strain on wives, who realize that their marriages are built on sand.

The unfaithful husband faces a perennial problem in finding a venue for his illicit liaisons: the beach at night is generally for the very young or very poor or very desperate. In recent years, however, there have appeared a number of establishments known as *hotéis de alta rotatividade*—hotels of high rotation—offering short-term accommodation for clandestine couples with nowhere to go. (Ordinary hotels in Rio do not allow guests to have visitors in their rooms.) The high-rotation hotels are located on the extreme edge of the city—at Barra da Tijuca and along the Rodovia Washington Luís on the way to Petrópolis—and are the product, so it has been said, of two important developments in the social life of Rio de Janeiro: the automobile and the pill. The high-rotation hotels quickly became the temples of adultery in the city, monuments in stone and steel and glass to the complex world of the affair. With high surrounding walls and a single entrance, Hollywood-kitsch architecture (desert oasis, romantic castle), exotic pink and mauve exterior floodlighting, and bedrooms equipped with ceiling mirrors and slowly revolving beds, they offer a secure and luxurious ambience for the pursuit of the Carioca's most noble and constant pastime.

A predilection for beautiful women is one of the few immutable elements in Carioca life. Fashions in female beauty come and go, however. The ideal of female sexuality is now the *garôta*, the teenager who is half-girl, half-woman. For a brief moment in her life this nymph achieves a per-fection of flesh and form that remains for ever the envy of her less fortunate dumpling elders. The *garôta's* figure is firm and lissom and almost uni-sexual in character: that is to say, the emphasis on the organs of gestation and lactation, the womb and the breasts, is diminished. The ideal *garôta* is small-breasted, flat-tummied, apple-bottomed—a love-object rather than a mother figure. From street hoardings and magazines model girls turn their buttocks towards the camera and you in a blatantly suggestive fashion. At high-society Carnival balls this posteriorizing in front of photo-graphers is almost *de rigueur*, a cliché to rival the pouted lips and the frontal shot of previous years.

The emphasis on youth in Carioca sexuality puts exceptional pressure on the women of Rio to rejuvenate and to improve their looks. In a city

A restaurant in downtown Rio (above) offers take-away portions of feijoada completa—a mixture of black beans, minced meat and rice that ranks as the national dish—and displays two containers just to make the message clear. On the right, a shoe-repair and key-cutting kiosk advertises its services even more graphically, perhaps hoping to attract some of the city's estimated 300,000 illiterates.

where appearance is more important than substance and where most of the chic rich spend half their time nearly naked in public—on the beach, on the yacht, by the pool, at the Carnival ball—the cult of the body beautiful has become an obsession. There are more than a thousand beauty parlours in Rio and more than a score of plastic surgery clinics that handle major alterations of the human contours. These clinics are the dream palaces of Rio, where the old and the ugly and the undesirable re-emerge miraculously transformed, their noses shortened, jowls lifted, eye-bags smoothed, bellies flensed, hips scoured, breasts made smaller and buttocks pumped up.

So great is the demand for beauty that the plastic surgeons, colloquially known as *plásticos*, have waxed exceedingly rich. The most legendary among them is Dr. Ivo Pitanguy. Dr. Pitanguy's success spawned the entire plastic surgery boom. He is accepted as the grand master of his profession, and his handiwork is approved by observers with the kind of critical admiration usually reserved for inanimate works of art. Connoisseurs pride themselves on their ability to spot, at a distance, a Pitanguy nose. In his private life the doctor is everything that a Carioca might aspire to be, a man whose material and personal success is as fabulous as James Bond's. He owns three magnificent houses—one near Rio, one on a private tropical island down the coast, another in Switzerland—with saunas, swimming pools, tennis courts, speedboats, a private airstrip. He practises karate and judo, skis, scuba dives around the world, speaks six languages and reads the classics. Dr. Pitanguy is one of Rio's latter-day miracle-makers in a city that believes in miracles.

One of the few concerns to rival sex and the body beautiful in Rio is soccer, which has an enormous and fervent following. The sport is still young in Brazil. It was introduced at the turn of the century by a certain Charles Miller, a Brazilian of British stock who had been sent to England to complete his education. He returned an enthusiastic convert to the sport he had played at school, and set about organizing games among his friends. His enthusiasm was infectious. Soccer rapidly attracted a coterie of supporters, and the Rio Football League was founded in 1906.

The new game that was nurtured under the palm trees and the warm equatorial skies of Brazil soon bore little relationship to the kind of game that was played in the wintry industrial towns of Britain. True, many English words of soccer terminology were absorbed into the Brazilian language, like *gol* (goal); *goleiro* (goalie); *pênalti*; *chutar* (to shoot); *time* (pronounced teemee, meaning team); and the word *futebol* itself. But while the British game evolved into a form of ritualized tribal warfare, with the hard physical contest on the field paralleled by the even bloodier struggle between the fans in the stands, the Brazilian game became a sporting show, a competitive exhibition of artistry and skill. While the

The Many Faces of Rio

A wide spectrum of racial pigmentation is seen in Rio's population—a legacy of centuries of interbreeding between people of European, African and Amerindian stock. A whole vocabulary exists to describe the features of those inhabitants who cannot simply be classed as black or white. It ranges from general terms like *mestiço* (of mixed race) and *caboclo* (of Indian and Portuguese blood) to words defining specific groups such as the *morenos* (dark whites) and the *cabosverdes* (straight-haired Negroes).

The random survey of faces on the right reveals one nearly universal characteristic of Cariocas—a deep-dyed zest for pleasure. From the wistful smile of a long-time favela resident (centre row, second from left) to the broad grin of a sun-visored beach-goer (top row, centre), the expressions are those of a people who know how to enjoy life.

British players laid most emphasis on matiness and group solidarity—the famous team spirit that won empires and bred bomber crews—the Brazilian players regarded themselves as virtuosos in a loose confederation that shared a common aim. While the British coined a whole jargon to define techniques of physical collision—barge, tackle, body check, block, put the boot in—the Brazilians invented a new range of skills to extend the relationship between man and ball: the amazing banana kick, the overhead backward bicycle kick, the back-of-the-heels flip-on, and an elaborate repertoire of dribbles, swerves, and feints. It is these skills that have made Brazil one of the supreme football nations in the world, frequent winners of the World Cup and home of Pelé, perhaps the greatest soccer player of all time; and it is the Rio clubs that provide the principal arena for the national game.

The first football match I saw in Rio was also the first of the new season and one of the best: the traditional opener called the Fla-Flu, between the old rival clubs Flamengo and Fluminense, whose teams include some of the finest players in Brazil. The match was played in the huge Maracanã Stadium—a vast circle of concrete enclosing a smaller circle of evening sky, with a sickle moon in the centre and bats fluttering around the edge. The concrete terraces had had the sun on them all day and were almost too hot to sit on; a great many men in the crowd were stripped to the waist.

The result of the match was of no great consequence to me. As it happened Flamengo won 4-1, mainly due to the outstanding brilliance of a young forward who was hailed as the new Pelé and scored all of Flamengo's four goals, a record for one player in the 70 years of Fla-Flu encounters. What interested me most about the match, however, was the psychological background to the event, not only among the players but also among the crowd.

I watched the match in the company of an American friend who had never seen a soccer match before. This gave me the opportunity to foist upon her my nascent views of the Brazilian game. As the complex pattern of play unfolded on the field beneath us, I struggled to find adjectives that would properly describe the essence of what I saw—an exercise as clumsy as trying to define the bouquet of fine wines. The words I eventually found were the following: uninhibited, happy, plastic, round, rubbery, bendy, surging, pulsing, throbbing, explosive, hallucinogenic, feline. By contrast, it seemed to me, European-style football was planned, uptight, dour, angular, jagged, stiff, attrition-like, down-to-earth, canine. Those were the words I used—crude verbal grape-shot to pepper an elusive target. But such epithets do, I think, illuminate the extraordinary sense of fun that is engendered by a group of Brazilians doing something they enjoy.

The crowd at the Fla-Flu match contained a very large middle-class element. The spectators were good-humoured and well-behaved, although also very noisy and exuberant. They waved huge coloured banners and

Showing good form, a young soccer enthusiast scores a goal in a courtyard that doubles as the practice ground for Carnival musicians and dancers from the Mangueira favela. The sign on the wall informs visitors that the Mangueira percussion band wishes them all a happy Christmas and a prosperous New Year.

beat samba rhythms on drums throughout the entire match. The uproar never for a moment flagged to *sotto voce*, still less to silence. It was impossible to hear the referee's whistle either at the start or end of the match, and during an attacking move, or when a goal was scored, the noise surged like the revving of a jet's engines when it prepares for take-off.

Although the behaviour of the people around me was spirited and extrovert, it was never violent. When Flamengo scored their second goal, a wag behind me yelled, "Flamengo could do this with their hands tied behind their backs, but they don't want to be too cocky!" No shouts of "Flamengo swine!" greeted this inflammatory remark, no beer bottle was broken across the man's skull. When Flamengo scored their third goal, he cried out, "Flamengo aren't going to score any more; they don't want to make Fluminense squirm!" And when they scored their fourth, his excitement was so great that he picked up the nearest object available—a tiny transistor radio belonging to a Fluminense supporter listening to the radio commentary of the match—and hurled it over the terrace into the crowd below. Whether the little radio hit someone or not, I do not know. But in the immediate vicinity, at least, no bloodshed resulted from this importunity. "I am very sorry," he said simply to its owner; "I'll pay." And the matter was settled without even a voice raised in anger, let alone blows. Given the excitement aroused by the Fla-Flu match, it was a wonderful lesson in self-control.

This surprising lack of aggression is a noteworthy feature of the Carioca personality. The Brazilian does not instinctively resort to violence when he feels slighted or wronged, and the Carioca especially is renowned for his patience, tolerance and good humour in spite of the growing difficulties of urban existence. There is, heaven knows, enough violence in Rio, perpetrated both by criminals and police, but the passivity of the great majority of the people is sufficiently widespread for it to be a topic for debate even among themselves.

One aspect of the Cariocas' tolerance is a readiness to accept strangers arriving from other parts of Brazil or from abroad. Rio is a hospitable city. The authorities have a reputation for unwillingness to extradite wanted men at the behest of foreign governments, and ever since the time that the Prince Regent of Portugal fled to Rio, the city has been the refuge of exiles and escapees of all kinds and persuasions. Many of the exiles have been very successful in their country of adoption. For example, Hans Stern—a Jew who fled from Nazi Germany with his family when he was only 16—became the jewel king of Brazil, handling 70 per cent of the country's trade in precious stones. His firm is one of the top four jewellery businesses in the world.

The best-known of Rio's exiles may well be Ronald Biggs, an English-man who took part in what has been called the crime of the century. Biggs was a member of a 19-man gang that in 1963 relieved a Glasgow-London mail train of £2$\frac{1}{2}$ million worth of bank notes returning to the Bank of England for pulping. Not long after the crime Biggs was arrested, along with 12 others. He was sentenced to 30 years' imprisonment but had served little more than a year of his sentence when he escaped from jail. His fugitive odyssey took him to Paris for plastic surgery and then to Australia, where he lived in respectable anonymity for nearly five years until the police were tipped off and he was forced to flee to South America. Biggs decided to settle in Rio, a city he had fancied ever since he saw a picture of Botafogo Bay and Sugar Loaf mountain in an airline catalogue. He moved into Copacabana and, with his talent for adaptation, soon started to learn the Carioca way of life. He thereupon became an endless source of speculation and gossip among Brazilians and visitors alike.

The idea of a master criminal marooned on a tropic shore, surrounded by brown-skinned girls beneath waving palms is an intriguing one, and I was sufficiently intrigued myself to set off in search of the master crook's lair. I finally found him in a quiet seaside resort 50 miles down the coast from Rio. He was staying at his weekend home—a comfortable but modest place, suggesting that not very much was left of the £150,000 that constituted his share of the robbery spoils. Biggs was in bed with his girl friend when I arrived. As I stood at the garden gate, his face—oddly familiar to me from all the newspaper photographs I had seen—appeared at the open upstairs bedroom window.

"Hello, mate," he said. "I'll be down in a tick."

His face disappeared, then reappeared a second or two later.

"On second thoughts," he added, "make it ten minutes. There's a beer in the fridge. Make yourself at home."

Rio's newest sport, autobol, is a volatile blend of two Cariocan passions: soccer and fast driving. Teams of up to five drivers try to bump an outsized ball into the opponents' net—although, as the battered sides of this vehicle indicate, the contestants spend almost as much time bumping each other's cars.

When he eventually appeared, tall, barefoot and buttoning up his shirt, he struck me as younger and more debonair than his greying temples would suggest. Plastic surgery had had the effect not only of disguising his appearance, but of improving his looks as well. I was not surprised that women in Rio were among Biggs's best friends.

"I like it here very much," Biggs told me, talking quietly, almost shyly, in a carefully enunciated southern English accent. "I was driving past one day and decided it was where I wanted to live: quiet, clean beach, no hustle. So I rented this place in a girl friend's name. I pay 1,200 cruzeiros a month for it. But it's going up 40 per cent soon, and I may have to look for somewhere smaller. I'm not allowed to work in Brazil, you see. So I get a bit left behind when wages go up to compensate for inflation. It's difficult, money, no doubt about that."

Biggs's status as a marooned man of leisure was threatened soon after his arrival by his lack of proper papers. Faced with inevitable arrest, he tried to raise money for his family by selling his story to the London *Daily Express*. The paper tipped off Scotland Yard, and two British police officers were promptly dispatched to Rio to arrest him. But the Yard men never got Biggs back to Britain. Instead they became hopelessly ensnared in the quicksands of Brazilian bureaucracy. As much to Ronald Biggs's surprise as their own, they discovered that a little-known Brazilian law prevented any father of a Brazilian child from being extradited to another country against his will.

"By some miracle," Biggs told me, "I'd got this nightclub dancer bird of mine in the family way. I mean, I was going to be a Brazilian father."

Biggs was placed under a deportation order stipulating that he could be deported only to a country with no extradition treaty with Britain: in

practice this meant Venezuela and Costa Rica, and neither would accept him. The Yard men returned home empty-handed.

"All thanks to little Mikezinho here," said Biggs, indicating his toddler son who was happily tottering around the verandah and sipping beer from our glasses. "Where would I be now if it wasn't for this little bugger? I'll tell you where. Wandsworth Prison. And you ask me how I like Rio? Paradise on earth, mate. If I'd known then what I know now I'd have got straight off the plane when I got here and gone and got a bird in the pudding club right away."

Biggs's affection for Rio was absolutely genuine. The informality and the easy-going life suited him. But it was not a straightforward existence. For the time being, he was stateless, workless, penniless and cut off from his family and homeland. I left him alone on the verandah, with little Mike chortling around his chair—one of Rio's more colourful refugees sitting under a maracujá tree on the Tropic of Capricorn, 6,000 miles from home and with 28 years of a jail sentence still to run.

Biggs's experience with the British police in Rio exemplifies a quality that plays an important part in the Carioca's daily life. It is known as *jeito*, a word that cannot be translated exactly, but which means a knack or aptitude for fixing something, getting around some problem, coming out on top. With it, the Carioca is able to serve his own ends without resorting to the kind of aggression he finds so distasteful. Ronald Biggs, by pure good fortune, happened to have it; the British police did not, and this was a fatal drawback, for the whole of Rio runs on *jeito*, just as Republican Rome used to run on honour and duty. When a Carioca tells you. *"Não tem jeito"*—that he hasn't got it—it means that he is in a very bad way.

Every New Year's Eve, office-workers in Rio celebrate the end of the year by emptying old files out of their windows—and adding toilet rolls or computer print-outs for good measure. The results, as seen above in Praça Pio X, are a street-cleaner's nightmare but a source of great sport for the younger set.

Jeito can take many forms, but its results are always the same. The man who has it is the man who avoids the snares of life, while his *jeito*-less fellow-citizens are overwhelmed by them. A friend of mine in Rio has *jeito* in abundance. The man is a true Carioca in every respect, including his driving, which is to say that he drives recklessly, with an almost total lack of concern for his own life or that of other road-users. One day the inevitable happened: he caused a pile-up involving several cars in a busy street. The accident was almost entirely the result of his own reckless driving, yet when he told me about it he was grinning. I asked him why he seemed so happy about it. "I was the only driver whose papers were in order," he explained. "The police booked all the other drivers and let me go. My insurance company will foot the repair bill."

So crucial is *jeito* in everyday life in Rio that there are even professional *jeito* experts called *despachantes*, little men with attaché cases who will hire their services out to you as customs brokers or driving-licence brokers or visa brokers, and will facilitate your passage through the uncharted reefs and shoals of the city's omnipresent bureaucracy when you have no *jeito* of your own. As far as I know, the Brazilian *despachante* is unique in the world. In a few hours he will magically cut through all the red tape and official obfuscation that could hold you up for weeks.

I can vouch for the effectiveness of customs *despachantes* from my own experience on several visits to Rio as a working journalist. I was faced with the problem of getting expensive photographic equipment past the grasping hands of Rio's customs officials, who are among the biggest powers in the land. The first time, I attempted to do so by following the officially approved bureaucratic procedure. I approached the customs desk armed with an elaborate document signed by the Brazilian Consul-General in London; this document explained at length that the cameras and lenses were necessary working equipment, as defined under the terms of technical and cultural agreements signed between the governments of Brazil and Great Britain. The customs officer was unimpressed. The cameras were confiscated, and I had to pay a large security bond to get them back. On the second visit, I simply put myself and my cameras in the hands of a *despachante*. "No problem," he said. "All you will have to do is to hang around until just about noon. Then the officers will begin to feel hungry, and you'll have no trouble." Sure enough, as noon approached, an abstracted, preoccupied look came over the customs men and they behaved with the restless impatience of deprived addicts. "Now is the time!" whispered my little *despachante*. The customs officers had no wish to prolong their agonies a minute longer and they impetuously waved me through.

The *despachante* is an institutionalized form of what anthropologists call functional friendship—that is, friendship for a reason other than affection or regard. Functional friendship is one of the most important sorts of human relationship in Rio. The Brazilian, for all his hail-fellow-well-met air, never wholly trusts anyone. Usually his friends are members of a functional friendship network who are carefully chosen for their power to help, to intercede in key places, if the need arises: it is the only way to beat the system. This network is assiduously maintained—hence the apparent *bonhomie*, the huge parties in one another's houses, the generous gifts of flowers, records or chocolates, the constant check on the level of friendship ("Why haven't you rung me in the last two weeks? What has destroyed our friendship?"). The tremendous warmth of the Carioca is thus a formula for survival, and every friendship has its pay-off.

The element of self-interest in the Carioca's amiability does not diminish his appetite for other people's company. Every so often this need will express itself in a moment of intense conviviality that, once experienced, is not easily forgotten. I remember a night in a pavement restaurant by the sea, still packed and serving out steaks and wine at 4 o'clock in the morning, when a young man and woman at a near-by table began to play guitars. An old street busker with a mandolin joined in, and everyone burst out singing and beating dinner plates with their knives and forks. The guitarists worked expertly down the finger-board in semitone steps through the strange, off-key harmonies of Brazilian *batucada* music: E flat 7th and the 5th of A to the 7th of A flat minor. The waiters and the shoeshine boys and the tarts and the vendors of toy clowns and mechanical monkeys on the pavement outside stopped and listened and began to sing too, and for a moment it seemed that time was standing still and we were preserved like ants in amber in the magic atmosphere of *joie de vivre* and brotherly love forever.

The next morning, of course, all such emotions had vanished like snow in the Copacabana sun. The Carioca needs no reminding of the transience of happiness, for one side of his nature is definitely melancholy. To anyone arriving in Rio for the first time and indoctrinated in the city's public image of happiness and fun, the occasional melancholy of the Carioca comes as a surprise. Although the Carioca does not suffer from melancholy as severely as some of his compatriots, he suffers nonetheless. In part, this melancholy derives from that famous Portuguese emotion known as *saudade*, the sadness of nostalgia and longing, for which no single satisfactory word exists in English; but Carioca *saudade* falls with sudden intensity, generally when it is raining, and in normal circumstances it clears up almost as rapidly—as soon as the sun comes out.

There is nothing particularly inconsistent about the melancholy of the lighthearted Carioca; the archetypal court fool was always in reality the most earnest man in the kingdom. The Carioca is a manic depressive, a man of fits and starts, a creature of moods, of spontaneous volition. There is no continuity in his behaviour; instead there is an irregular rhythm in

A long-haired exponent of the martial art of capoeira leaps over his opponent during a bout on a Rio lawn. This balletic form of unarmed combat originated when the slaves of Brazil, forbidden to fight by their masters, learned to disguise their conflicts as dances. Capoeira was banned until the early 20th Century, but is now a popular sport.

which the Carioca, under the stimulus of some emotional shock, changes suddenly from a state of indolence to one of impetuous activity, from withdrawal and abstraction to feverish participation. This power to react, to tap hidden reserves of energy when least expected, can be very puzzling to visitors, but then the Carioca will always remain something of a mystery to outsiders who venture on to his home ground.

The eccentricities of life in Rio for a foreigner have been precisely and hilariously defined by Peter Kellemen, a post-war Hungarian immigrant who wrote a book called *Brasil para Principiantes* (*Brazil for Beginners*), a best-seller in its time. Even before he arrived in the country of his adoption, Mr. Kellemen learned not only of *jeito*, the first and most important adjunct of daily life in Brazil, but also of the *código secreto*, the secret code, the second most important adjunct.

"You will adore everything," said the doctor who gave him his vaccinations in Paris before he set off—a man who had lived in Rio for 20 years. "What a country! What women! However, you must learn not only Portuguese, but the secret code. Learn to interpret gestures, half-words, glances, insinuations; and you must always remember that the Brazilian will never use the word 'No'.

"Temporarily you will get lost in a vast labyrinth where 'Tomorrow' means 'Never'; where 'Come over to my place' doesn't constitute an invitation; where 'God willing I will come' means 'Don't count on seeing me'; where 'I've just made arrangements' means 'I haven't done a thing about it, I don't know what it's all about anyway'; and where 'We'll give you a call when your application comes through' means, 'Your application is at the bottom of my in-tray, don't ever bother me again'. But eventually, after a temporary period of apparent insanity, you will understand the secret code and be able to behave like a Brazilian."

After a few years of trial and error, Peter Kellemen learned the essential behaviour traits so well that he could pass himself off as a Brazilian. Among these traits were the following:

"Slap everybody on the back and cordially embrace all the people you meet, calling them 'My son' irrespective of age.

"When you come across an unaccompanied woman, always murmur something incomprehensible but flattering; if she is accompanied by a weedy-looking man, it is enough to give her an amorous look; if she is accompanied by a tough-looking man, leave it for another day.

"If you see a crowd gathered in the street because of some accident or disaster, always join it and immediately offer your opinion, pointing out the real culprit and indicating the action the others must take.

"Instead of the word 'No', use 'More or less', 'It's difficult', or 'Could be'."

So hard is it to behave as a Carioca that even Cariocas are uncertain how to go about it. To try to cast some light on their paradoxicality, I went to question a man who, as a cartoonist and painter, had devoted a good part of his life to studying his fellow-citizens' comportment.

Augusto Rodrigues, it turned out, lived in one of the most unusual and coveted homes in the whole of Rio, facing on the little 18th-Century-style square called the Largo do Boticário. It was a hot morning, so we went out to the long first-floor verandah, which looks over the square's shady wild fig trees and sprays of bamboo, its fluttering butterflies and yellow birds and its backdrop of forested hills. We sat in chairs carved out of huge single chunks of brazilwood. Overhead were elaborate wooden birdcages and hammocks furled like sails. At increasingly frequent intervals, Augusto would fetch large bottles of beer from the refrigerator. The beer seemed to loosen the workings of his mind; as he warmed to his theme, epigrams and jokes fell pell-mell from his mouth like coins from a fruit machine.

"Carioca? Carioca?" Augusto was saying. "What is that? Who is he? To understand the Carioca you must first understand the Paulista. Why? Because São Paulo has no beach. São Paulo is the Milan of Brazil. Rio is the Rome, without the ruins. To become a Carioca is just possible for a Paulista if he gives up worldly ambition; it is just possible for someone from Bahia if he gives up peace of mind; it is just possible for the Pernambucano after years of acclimatization. But for the foreigner it is almost impossible, because the Carioca is insane: he has to be to drink rum and eat black beans in this climate.

"An Englishman can't become a Carioca. He is too conscientious, he has a code, he never goes anywhere without his walking stick, even if it is only in his mind. The Argentinian can't become a Carioca; he is an Italian who speaks Spanish and thinks he is an Englishman—a hopeless case. Every time an Italian says one word he uses five gestures, every time an Englishman says five words he uses no gestures, but a Carioca, you see, uses ten words and ten gestures and means nothing, and that is a difficult form of expression to learn. Let me get some more beer."

One reason why the Carioca finds it difficult to explain his fellow-citizens to outsiders is that at heart he remains something of a mystery to himself. As a result, he is often thrown back on the expedient of telling jokes whose theme is that the Carioca is impossible to understand, if not simply impossible. One joke goes back to the very fount of things: the Creation. God, the story goes, is busy making the world. When it comes to Rio's turn, God really warms to his work and creates a magnificent bay, majestic mountains, a wonderful tropical forest, breathtaking beaches, grassy plains, a benign climate, glorious nights, brilliantly coloured birds and butterflies, and seas teeming with fish. By the time he has finished, he has created the most beautiful scenery on earth. The inhabitants of other places in the world are aghast. "It is grossly unfair," says a delegation sent to remonstrate with God. "Some of our places have got next to nothing, but Rio has been given everything."

"Ah," says God, giving them the wink. "Don't worry, my friends. Wait till you see the *people* I am going to put there."

Such jokes, I hasten to point out, in no way diminish the Carioca's profound spirit of patriotism, his total adoration of his beloved city and his native land. "God is a Brazilian" is a traditional saying that neatly crystallizes the Brazilian's ambivalence on this point: on the one hand supreme self-confidence, and on the other gnawing self-doubt—for how would they get by if He were not?

Peerless Pleasure Grounds by the Sea

By midday, Copacabana beach is thronged almost to capacity as Cariocas stroll in the sun, cool themselves in the water or seek refuge beneath umbrellas.

Few spots on earth are so richly endowed with opportunities for seaside pleasure as Rio. From the bays along Guanabara Bay, through the great skyscraper-lined Atlantic sweeps of Copacabana and Ipanema, to the near-wild coastline of the south-west, the fine sands of two dozen beaches extend for at least 50 miles. The beaches have a multitude of uses. They are temples for the Rio religion of body awareness and sun-worship, settings for ball games and courtship, playgrounds for children, comfortable places to transact business, or simply somewhere to sleep. Above all, they are the natural arenas for the Cariocas' irrepressible gregariousness. Upwards of 100,000 people flock to Copacabana on summer weekends, spurning emptier beaches to pack this magnificent stretch of sand more tightly than the city's busiest shopping streets.

A couple commune beside the mild early morning waves at Leblon beach, while a well-wrapped gentleman gets the blood moving with dignified knee-bends.

Near the sinuous mosaic pattern of the Avenida Atlântica, kites await purchasers, and a pair of youngsters warm up for a daily football contest.

Exercising the dog along the two and a half miles of Copacabana beach is as much part of the chic scene as ownership of a seaview apartment or a perfect tan.

A pretty Carioca girl shows how the fashionable tanga, or micro-bikini, should be worn in Rio: not just too small, but 10 sizes too small.

At a beachside café, a macho male turns in his chair to indulge in a favourite Carioca pastime: girl-watching.

Tidying her partner's hair, a sunbather indulges the love of physical contact common to all Rio's beach-goers.

5

Mysteries of the Spirit Cults

A young Carioca wears an exotic headdress of metalwork and beads during a ceremony that will qualify her to communicate with the deities of Candomblé, one of the Afro-Brazilian spiritist religions practised in Rio. The beads are meant to protect her against evil influences.

To the casual eye, Rio would appear to be an entirely Catholic city, deeply immersed in the faith brought over by the first Portuguese colonists in the days of the Inquisition. It is a city of many fine old churches and cathedrals, where mass is celebrated regularly and the feast days of the Catholic calendar are punctiliously observed; it is also a city where almost every citizen at almost any hour of day or night can observe the ethereal statue of Christus Redemptor on Corcovado, a towering symbol of the established faith of the nation.

But first impressions are deceptive. A visitor soon becomes aware of another, quite different sort of religious zeal at work within the city—a widespread commitment to a variety of spiritist cults involving magic rites and spells. On pavements, at crossroads, and along the beaches you will frequently see candles flickering far into the night; and beside the candles bottles of rum, unlit cigars and bowls of food placed there as gifts to the spirit world. In smart shopping streets in Copacabana and the city centre you will come across well-stocked shops doing a brisk trade in magic herbs and soaps, incense and love potions, crystal balls and tarot cards, jaguar and alligator teeth, bats' wings and dried cockroaches. Statuettes of Christian saints are also on sale there, alongside those of unfamiliar divinities: mermaids and luridly painted devils, old black men with turbans and Amerindians in war-paint. You will see any day, too, cradled between the breasts of the lovely girls on Ipanema beach, necklaces bearing good-luck charms called *figas*—each one a small clenched fist with a protruding thumb. And at any hour on Rio radio or in a corner café, you are likely to hear samba songs with lyrics such as: "Saravá, Nana e Oxumaré, Xangô, Oxóssi, Oxalá e Yemanjá"—a salutation to the spirit gods in the old tongues of the African slaves.

I had always known that some kind of spirit religion was practised in Rio. I had imagined that it was a fringe phenomenon, involving only the poorer members of Carioca society. It was not until I went to the cemetery of Inhaúma one midnight that I discovered how wrong I was. The cemetery is situated in the North Zone at the foot of the Serra da Misericórdia. It is a desolate spot, fronted by rubbish-strewn urban waste-land and a busy arterial road where the Rio traffic drones into the night. I was taken there by the son of a priest of the Umbanda cult, the biggest and fastest-growing spiritist cult in Rio. At Inhaúma, he told me when we set off, we would see Umbanda's darker side, a subsidiary cult known as Quim-banda, which is based on the practice of black magic. In the cemetery were said to live two of the most fearsome members of the spiritist pantheon: the Devil, or Exú, and his woman, the prostitute known as Pomba Gira.

All along the pavement outside the cemetery wall burned scores of candles and through the railings I could see many more flickering in the blackness among the gravestones. The candles had been purchased from a young woman who sat against the wall near the cemetery gate, while her six-year-old daughter lay asleep on the paving stones. She was there every night from 7 in the evening to 5 the next morning, and there was never any lack of customers who wanted to burn a candle and make an offering to the Exú in return for his help with one problem or another.

A score of such customers stood singly or in groups along the pavement, their faces intent and anxious in the candlelight. One small group conversed in conspiratorial voices with a man stripped to the waist and swathed in beads; he was a specialist in black magic, my guide informed me, and was spelling out the exact procedure that they would have to follow to propitiate the Devil. Others stood in front of offerings they had already made to the Devil: a curious scattering of consumer goods and animal sacrifices that covered the pavement for some 50 yards.

Almost anything that was considered to be to the Devil's liking was laid out for his perusal. There were bowls of tomatoes and onions and rice, pots of stew, and strings of smoked sausages. Many cigars were scattered about, along with countless bottles of the Devil's favourite drink, the raw sugar-cane spirit called *cachaça*, whose oily alcoholic stench, mixed with the smoke of burning candle wax, hung in the air. Here and there, larger bowls contained the corpses of black chickens with their throats cut and their blood spattered over the ground. In one basin, the severed head of a goat lay marinating in its own blood; its sightless eyes gleamed like polished stones in the candlelight.

The scene at Inhaúma that midnight was not a little unnerving. But what astonished me was not so much the procedural details of black magic and animal sacrifice as the status of the participants. Many were educated, wealthy, white and upper-class people who were smartly dressed and had arrived in expensive motor cars. I was particularly intrigued by one white family—a mother, two grown-up sons, and two grown-up daughters— who seemed to be in the grip of some tragedy. They were too tense and earnest for me to ask them what had brought them there and made them attempt this extreme measure of supernatural intervention, and I could only guess that the father, who was notably absent from the group, was suffering from some serious illness. Perhaps the family hoped that by placating the Exú they might drive the illness away.

As I watched, one of the daughters, dressed as if she were going to a fashionable first night at the theatre, approached a lavish set of gifts laid out on the pavement and placed whole bundles of candles beside the offerings. When all the candles were lighted, she picked up a bottle of

At a news kiosk, pictures of spiritist divinities such as the Old Black Slave (far left) and Yemanjá (third from left) are offered alongside Christian icons.

cachaça and with ritual deliberation smashed it on the ground. Three times more she did this, until the air reeked with the odour of strong alcohol. As she broke the fourth bottle, the inflammable spirit splashed over the candles and ignited. Licking blue flames crept among the bowls of food laid out for the Devil's enjoyment, setting the cigars alight and singeing the black feathers of a headless chicken. While the fire followed the course of the spilt *cachaça* towards the gutter, the young woman scattered pop-corn—the Devil's favourite delicacy, my companion told me—amid the smouldering debris, and the rest of the family looked on with bowed heads and grave expressions. ●

How long they might have stayed there contemplating their bizarre offering I do not know. But when the flames reached the gutter, all the paper and rubbish in it caught fire and threatened to engulf the family's car in an even greater conflagration. In silence, and with faces still tragic, the family retreated from the Devil's pavement and drove off. After they had gone, urchins from a neighbouring favela began to play with the burning rubbish, and a tramp propped against the cemetery wall laughed demoniacally among the shadows.

"Have you ever seen anything like that before?" my guide asked.

I said that I had witnessed something a little similar deep in the West African bush, but never had I seen well-to-do white people actively participating. It was, I said, a cultural shock.

"Here in Rio," he informed me, "everyone is taking part now—generals, government ministers, lawyers, architects, police chiefs, civil servants, pop stars, the rich and upper classes as well as the poorer illiterate people. Deep down, they all believe in magic and the supernatural."

It was then that I realized I would have to come to grips with spiritism before I could claim to understand Rio.

Spiritist practices and beliefs are extraordinarily confusing to an outsider. Every new discovery you make seems to raise a question or reveal a paradox. Not only do you notice Christian and pagan icons on sale in the same shops, but if you attend a session at a spiritist centre you will see the congregation and its leaders go into hysterical trances in front of altars set with images of Christ or the Virgin Mary. No less baffling is the nomenclature of spiritism and the hierarchy of the spirits: once you learn the names of some of the spirit gods you find that whole armies of lesser spirits are organized under them. But perhaps the most difficult task of all is to disentangle one set of spirit beliefs from another.

Non-believers, both foreigners and Brazilians, tend to lump the various cults together under the name Macumba, a popular term for spiritist practices. But in Rio the word has a derogatory ring and carries the implication that spiritists are primitive and barbaric. It is best to refer to each cult by its own name.

An open bottle of liquor, a cigar and a box of matches—left at the roadside to win favour from a spiritist god—remain untouched by Rio's superstitious citizenry long after a votive candle has burnt down to a crust of wax. Such offerings, called *despachos*, are often placed near crossroads—regarded as a particular haunt of the more sinister spiritist deities.

Broadly speaking, there are three main cults: Candomblé, Kardecism, and Umbanda (with Quimbanda as its sinister offshoot). Candomblé, the oldest of the cults, is descended from the Yoruba religion of West Africa. Kardecism owes nothing to Africa; it developed from a form of spiritism popular in 19th-Century France. Umbanda, the youngest and most Brazilian of the cults, is a synthesis of both Candomblé and Kardecism and has added several indigenous spirits of its own in the semblance of black slaves and Amerindians. However, because these main cults take different forms in different places and keep changing with time, spiritists will often simply define their practices as "working through the saints".

All three cults rest on the belief that men can make direct contact with spirits living in some other world and that those spirits can work for the welfare of men. At spiritist centres contact is made through the agency of human mediums who operate on special wavelengths, so to speak, and have their own guardian spirits. By various means, including drumming and singing, a particular spirit can be induced to come down from the astral realm and possess a medium, who then goes into a trance. While possessed, the medium provides the spirit with a temporary corporeal existence, adopting its voice and language and characteristic behaviour, and sometimes carrying out magical tasks.

When a spirit is present in the body of a medium, the members of the congregation are allowed to consult that medium and ask the spirit's help in solving their mortal problems. All manner of questions are posed during these consultations: how to cure an illness, regain a lost love, arrange a marriage, gain a job or promotion or settle a dispute with a maid (a common occurrence in the household affairs of Rio).

Frequently, people attend a spirit session when they are sick, hoping to find magical cures for illnesses they cannot afford to have treated through conventional medicine or that conventional medicine regards as incurable. It is in this role that the spiritist cults of Brazil receive their greatest publicity, for many remarkable operations by spirit healers have been reported, some of them attested by medical experts. According to these reports, people have been cured of cancer, the blind have been given sight and the crippled made to walk. Probably the most famous spirit healer in Brazil was José Arigó, killed in a car crash in 1971, who became known all over the country for his miraculous cures, and especially his eye operations. His surgical equipment consisted of kitchen knives, a scalpel, a pair of tweezers and a pair of scissors kept in an old tin can. Innumerable witnesses, including sceptical newsmen and medical specialists, watched him perform one of his most celebrated feats: taking one of his knives, he would scrape a patient's eyeball under the lid or even remove it altogether in order to get to the back of it, and although he used no anaesthetic, his patients seemed not to feel any pain. By such unconventional methods Arigó could apparently cure any kind of eye complaint with total success.

In Rio, a spectacular demonstration of Umbanda magic was transmitted live on one of the television channels. A well-known doctor from the north of Brazil, who had been unable to walk for years, was cured of his disability by an Umbanda priestess and walked off the stage under the eyes of seven medical specialists and a television audience of millions. Shortly before I arrived, a different but even more sensational demonstration of Umbanda power took place on another live television show: an Umbanda priestess, said to be possessed by a spirit named Seu Sete (Mister Seven), reduced half the audience to a hysterical, shrieking trance and deprived the man who chaired the show of his power of speech.

The same Cariocas who attend spirit sessions may also seek supernatural aid on their own, through private offerings to the gods. The offerings, known as *despachos*, are as varied as the supplicants' wishes and the number of gods in the spiritist pantheon. For example, if you are in love with someone who is not in love with you, you must pour *cachaça* over the base of a tree, place three candles in a row, write your loved one's name on the back of a photograph of yourself, then burn the photo in the flame of the centre candle. The fire will thus join your face and your loved one's name, and you will be together very shortly afterwards.

Such practices come under the broad heading of white magic, since they are benign in their intent. In black magic, you call on the Devil, or Exú, and get him to do evil for you. (Actually there are many Exús, all personifications of the Devil, with names such as Skull, Shadow, Crossed Path, Hot Ashes, and Pitchfork.) The methods of solicitation are predictably bizarre. If, for example, you wish to bring harm to an enemy, you must follow these instructions. First, get hold of a live black toad and sew up its mouth with black thread. Next, tie a long black thread to each of its toes and hang the toad upside down over a smoking fire. At midnight, spin the toad around and say, "Dirty toad, by the power of the Devil, stop So-and-So from having one more hour of happiness on earth. Toad, trap his health inside your mouth. Let him sicken and die." Next morning, put the toad in a jar and seal the lid with candle wax. If you wish to remove the curse, let the creature out of the jar before it dies, remove the stitches from its mouth, and give it fresh milk to drink for a week.

The practice of black magic is a serious matter, capable of producing gruesome results. A spiritist who believes he has received the Devil's instructions to harm or even murder an enemy may well carry out the evil deed, in case disobedience causes the evil to rebound upon himself. In consequence, black magic is illegal in Brazil; but since the police are as frightened of it as anyone else, little is ever done to enforce the law.

A redeeming feature of the Exús is that they may do good as well as evil; in fact, their aid is often sought for worthy causes. On the whole, the spiritist movement is positive in its effects as well as its intentions. In a country like Brazil where welfare services are minimal, the movement fulfils a valuable social need in providing faith-healing and emotional counselling. It even provides conventional social services, operating schools, orphanages and old people's homes which are financed by voluntary contributions.

The merits or demerits of spiritism can be debated endlessly, but there is no denying its success. More than 90 per cent of Brazilians describe them-selves as Catholics—yet many of them are also practising spiritists. Just how many it is impossible to know, because a large number will not openly admit they are believers; but responsible estimates of the total number of spiritists in Brazil vary from 5 to 20 million, roughly 5-20 per cent of the population. This makes Brazil the largest stronghold of spiritism in the world, as well as the largest Catholic nation. The spiritist movement is thoroughly entrenched in Rio. It can safely be assumed that between a fifth and a quarter of the city's inhabitants—more than a million people—at some time or other attend spiritist centres, of which there are probably upwards of 20,000, ranging from places where the spirits are appeased with animal sacrifices to high-brow establishments where the spirits are not even offered a bottle of cachaça.

Although the Catholic establishment in Brazil is implacably opposed to spiritism in all its forms, the Vatican has taken a rather different line. In a message published in 1967, Pope Paul VI declared that the Church must take a new look at the pagan religions of African origin and cherish those aspects that might bring about "a new approximation of the Church".

Without a doubt, spiritism owes much of its success to its syncretistic mixing of Christian and pagan rites and ceremonies. This blending was possible because of two features of early colonial society in Brazil: the religious adaptability of the African slaves and the mystical and magical leanings of their Portuguese masters.

Among the slaves shipped to Brazil from the mid-16th Century onwards, one of the dominant groups were the Yoruba of what is now Nigeria and Dahomey. Like other tribesmen, they brought with them a large pantheon of gods, a complex mythology and an elaborate system of ritual. Strictly speaking, the Portuguese colonial authorities did not permit the slaves to retain their pagan religions. Many of the Africans destined for servitude were baptized into the Christian faith as they stood in batches on the shores of their homeland waiting to be embarked on the slave ships; and in Brazil every slave owner was responsible for teaching Christianity to the people in his charge. But in practice the slaves merely observed the outward forms of Catholicism without undergoing any inner spiritual conversion.

This religious dualism was made easier by the convenient similarity between the Catholic hierarchy and the Yoruba pantheon. The chief god of the Yoruba religion, Olurun, was not represented by any totem or idol and had to communicate with men through a host of secondary divinities, called Orixás. Under the pressure of Catholic teaching, the Yorubas began

A Gallery of Devils

Of all the members of the spiritist pantheon, the divinities known as Exús inspire the greatest fear among believers. Roughly related to the Devil of the Christian faith, the Exús number in the hundreds. Each—as shown by the figurines on the right—has its own distinct traits, and each is partnered by a brazenly sensual she-demon, the whore named Pomba Gira (below).

Some Exús work exclusively for evil, but most will oblige supplicants by performing either good or bad deeds, from curing an illness to punishing an unfaithful husband. In return for their services, the Exús demand sustenance from the world of mortals. The Exú who guards graveyards is particularly partial to raw beefsteak; others prefer a platter of popcorn or a fat cigar; and all are fond of alcoholic refreshment—muscatel, whisky, or the sugar-cane rum called *cachaça*.

A double-headed Exú offers supplicants an androgynous brand of malignity.

A raven-haired Pomba Gira blends crude eroticism with trappings of royalty.

Carrying his trident before him, a bearded Exú is a vision of brute strength.

At once civilized and sinister, a black-hatted Exú complements his suave evening attire with an identifying necklace of black and red beads.

to associate their Olurun with God the Father in the Christian faith. Oxalá, the greatest Orixá and chief intermediary between man and Olurun, was easily seen to be Jesus Christ. Yemanjá, mother of the Orixás, was identified with Mary, the Mother of Christ. Similarly, the lesser Orixás were equated with the Christian saints. Ogun, god of war, was equated with St. George, and Oxóssi, the god of hunting, was identified with St. Sebastian, who had been shot to death with arrows. The Exús, who served as the messengers of the Orixás and did any dirty work that was necessary, were identified with the Devil of Christian lore.

By drawing on such parallels, the African priest in the slave barracks had no difficulty conducting services in his people's own religion while appearing to conduct them in the religion of his Portuguese masters. On the upper part of the altar he would place the images of the Catholic saints, but down below, away from the prying eyes of the authorities, he would place the effigies of the African gods.

The white Portuguese communities of the great plantations were easily influenced by their slaves' magical beliefs. Five centuries of subjection in Portugal to Muslim Moors from North Africa, combined with an acquaintance in the early years of Brazilian colonialism with the American Indian corpus of spiritist beliefs, had given them a considerable elasticity of religious consciousness. In addition, Portuguese Catholicism at this time retained much of its medieval mysticism—more so than the rest of Europe—and the Portuguese immigrants to Brazil had great faith in the magical healing powers of the saints and the evil powers of the Devil, both of which are basic to spiritism.

Out of the mixed religious experiences of the plantation owners of the 17th and 18th Centuries grew the religious ambivalence of the 20th-Century white Brazilian; and out of the Yoruba religion, with its Catholic parallels, grew the cult of Candomblé. The emergence of independent Candomblé centres was a strictly urban phenomenon. In 1830, the first known centre was set up in Bahia when three black freed-women took over a derelict old mill called the Engenho Velho and held Candomblé meetings there. In spite of the hostility of the Church establishment, this spiritist sanctuary flourished, and over the years more Candomblé centres were founded in Bahia making it the nucleus of Candomblé, which it has remained ever since. Many of the Bahian participants in Candomblé still use the Yoruba language—known in Brazil as Nagô. In Rio, other African languages from Angola and the Congo are more commonly spoken in Candomblé ceremonies and the cult's practitioners employ black magic more frequently than in Bahia.

Such variations from place to place can exist very easily, because every Candomblé group is autonomous—a separate, closed community obeying no outside authority and run with absolute power by a head priestess (Mãe de Santo, or Mother of Saint) or less often, a head priest (Pai de

A devout young Carioca, preparing to enter the Candomblé priesthood, gravely submits to having his shaven head drenched with the blood of a freshly sacrificed goat. Resting against his chest is an iron emblem symbolic of Oxóssi, the god of hunting.

White spots and lines painted on a girl's body during her initiation as a Candomblé medium represent the scars favoured by some African tribes as signs of beauty. According to the canons of the sect, mediums are able to summon up spirits that dwell on the shores of Africa.

Santo, or Father of Saint). The Mãe or Pai are attended by bevies of mediums called Filhos or Filhas de Santo (Sons or Daughters of Saint) who have been initiated into the mysteries by the Mãe or Pai personally.

The initiation ceremony lasts for several weeks. During this time the novice—usually female—is instructed in the secrets of Candomblé: how to sing and dance and beat the drums for the Orixás, how to read cowrie shells, how to make animal sacrifices and brew herbal potions, how to cook various spirit banquets. The initiation ceremony includes some highly charged and impressive rituals, in the course of which the Mother of Saint may make a small incision in the girl's scalp with a razor blade, and sacrifice a white duck and a white goat over her. When the sacrificial blood —human, animal and bird—has almost dried on her, she is bathed and daubed all over with spots of white paint, symbolic of the cicatrices of the African tribes of long ago. Then she is confined in a small room for three or four weeks, isolated from the everyday world.

But the most remarkable ritual is the final one. The initiates, their heads shaven and their bodies and faces still painted with white spots, are assembled in their full regalia of long satin and silk skirts, colourful scarves, African amulets to ward off the evil eye, necklaces of cowrie shells and a profusion of bangles and bracelets, and are taken by the Mother of Saint to hear Roman Catholic mass in the cathedral or church nearest to their Candomblé centre. Thus the crowning ceremony of one religion takes place in the most unlikely of places: the house of worship of another.

Most Candomblé sessions are held in specially constructed centres with good-sized gardens. A main building contains the assembly room for the dancers and drummers. At the rear of the assembly room is a corridor flanked by small side-chapels devoted to the various Orixás, and there may be numerous other rooms as well. Outside is an Exús' house, where the Devil can be given food and drink to keep him occupied during a session, and another house for the Eguns, the spirits of the dead.

My first contact with Candomblé was a visit to one of these centres in the North Zone, and I found it disturbing. The centre was a distinctly odd place, heavy with the atmosphere of black magic, the paraphernalia of the macabre and diabolical. I was uneasily aware of the immanence of evil— not the evil of some supernatural force, but an ordinary earthly evil.

The focus of my unrest was undoubtedly the leader of the centre. The Pai was the driving force of the whole place: he had founded it, he had created it in his own image. He was in his mid-30s, swarthy, good-looking and immensely enthusiastic and energetic. He was also charming, charismatic, polite and intelligent—yet I viewed him with profound suspicion.

"Tonight," he told me when I arrived at 9 one evening, "I am only doing work with the Devil. I am going to call him and he will come down some time after midnight. Would you like to see the house of the Exús?"

He took me to the nastiest place I had ever been in. The Exús' separate, one-room abode stood to the left of the front door and was like a little mausoleum. It smelt of death. The stench of putrefaction was so great that, even before I reached the door, I took very short breaths so that I would inhale as little of the air inside as possible. When we entered, there was a sudden razzmatazz of flies. The rotting corpses of chickens and squashed toads were scattered about a marked-off space at the back of the room, together with various unidentifiable and loathsome objects lying in bowls or hanging from hooks. On the walls were pinned crude coloured pictures of the spirits of Candomblé.

"Ninety per cent of the time," the Pai told me, "I do good. Ten per cent of the time I do evil. In order to combat evil I must do evil. I have a licence to kill, and from time to time I kill. What do you think of that? It was the Devil who gave me the right to kill. And I use the Devil's instrument of death." He stooped and picked up a trident—a three-pronged harpoon, about the same dimensions as a garden spade, with barbed points.

"You must understand, when I kill someone with this trident, it is to save the minds of ten people. Blood propitiates certain evil forces in the cosmos, so from time to time it is necessary to practise human sacrifice."

I wondered what exactly he meant by all this. Surely he was not really a killer? Was he simply trying to tell me what he thought I would like to hear? Or was he talking metaphorically, implying that he had the power to kill people through magic?

We went to the Casa dos Eguns, the house of the souls of the dead, opposite the Exús' house. It was a pleasant little room, furnished with an altar cross picked out in coloured light bulbs, and a little statuette of St. George on his horse and another of Christ crucified. There were candles and pink flowers strewn all over the floor and pictures of the sea and mountains on the wall. The Pai pointed out a little clay pot on a shelf.

"I keep 5,000 spirits of the dead in that pot," he explained. "They are all captive in my temple. They can't leave to trouble us."

We entered the main building. Immediately on the left was a room with a glass door and curtained windows. "This is the room of the Exú Tirirí Lonan. He is not so much the Devil as the King of the Kings of the Exús. I sometimes work with him, but not tonight." (Exú Tirirí Lonan is generally regarded by spiritists as a second-rank Devil, but every Pai runs his Candomblé centre in the way he pleases and this Pai had evidently decided to give his favourite Exú a promotion.) The room was like a peep-show at a fun-fair. Propped on a kind of throne surrounded by bottles of liquor was a lurid, life-size effigy of a Devil with a black goatee, a black top hat with a red band round it, a trident in his hand and a star-spangled cape over his shoulders. There was also an erotic and diabolical portrait of the Exú's woman, Pomba Gira, hanging on one wall, and an armchair with a plastic spittoon in the shape of a skull next to it—the devil's ashtray.

By the time I finished my tour of the various quarters, the centre was filling up for the evening session. The Pai excused himself and went to put on his robes. Since he intended to do secret work with the Devil that night, I was not allowed to stay. I turned and left to try my luck in the world of spiritism elsewhere in the city.

A brand of spiritism quite unlike Candomblé is Kardecism, named after a 19th-Century French school-teacher who wrote under the name of Allan Kardec. Kardec's seminal work, *The Book of Spirits*, describes supernatural phenomena associated with seances, the nature of life after death, voices from the other world and so on. The book was brought to Brazil by a Portuguese aristocrat in 1858, and since then Kardecism has gained many followers among the educated white sections of Brazilian society. Its adherents are particularly numerous in the more advanced cities such as Rio, where they are counted in tens of thousands.

Whereas the practitioners of Candomblé communicate only with the spirits of gods, Kardecists communicate only with the spirits of the dead. They teach that, on death, a person's spirit leaves the body and joins other disembodied spirits in some astral home. There it waits until, eventually, it is reincarnated in a new body. In the meantime, it can be called down, like the gods of Candomblé, to speak to the living.

The seances at which this calling down takes place are a world apart from Candomblé and its African drumming and chanting. The atmosphere is altogether European. The congregation are enjoined to keep silent, while the mediums sit round a table, dressed in white like hospital orderlies, and music by Gounod, Schubert or Chopin plays softly through a loudspeaker in the background. The mediums join hands and wait, until one of them is seized by a spirit and begins to speak with the spirit's voice. The leading medium then interviews the spirit, hoping to discover some details about its past life on earth.

Around this central activity of Kardecism has grown up a highly eclectic corpus of beliefs and practices that embrace elements of Christian teaching and 19th-Century amateur physics. As far as physics is concerned, Kardecists espouse a theory that the human body is surrounded by an aura of electrical or magnetic particles containing the soul or spirit, and that when people are ill, the aura is misshapen. It can be put back into order by a faith-healing process similar to the fundamentalist Christian practice of the laying on of hands: a medium replaces damaged particles in the aura with good particles radiating from his hands. Many cures have been claimed for this method—and no doubt it does work to the extent that people sincerely believe they will make a full recovery.

As far as spiritual well-being is concerned, Kardecists refer constantly to the teachings of Christ, especially that people should love one another. Each human spirit is reincarnated many times, they say, in a gradual

At the climax of an Umbanda meeting, dazed and writhing mediums (above) submit to the grip of the spirits, while the celebrant on the right seeks a similar state of entrancement with the aid of a ritual cigar, magical beads and ornaments and a white rose that is one of the symbols of her guardian deity.

evolution towards a state of perfection; but the evolution proceeds only if good works are performed in each lifetime. From the Kardecist belief in the transmigration of souls springs what is undoubtedly the cult's most powerful message: there is no death.

I was interested in Kardecism only to the extent that it helped me to comprehend Umbanda, Rio's biggest cult. Umbanda, which began to emerge in Rio as a distinct cult in the 1930s, is a compromise between the rarefied intellectual atmosphere of Kardecism and the noisy African-influenced rituals of Candomblé. Like Kardecism, Umbanda recognizes the concepts of reincarnation and communication with the spirits of the dead. Like Candomblé, it works through a pantheon of Orixás and Exús—although its chief god is Oxalá, or Jesus Christ, not Olurun, or God the Father—and it often relies in its rituals on drumming, singing and dancing, using African rhythms. Umbanda likewise uses magic charms and spells, and its priests and priestesses are also called Pai de Santo and Mãe de Santo, with Pais the more common.

Umbanda has at least 30 sects offering a range of rituals, from those most like Candomblé to those most like Kardecism, and it has been attracting greater numbers of middle- and upper-class Cariocas every year. It has two obvious advantages over Candomblé: first, many of its gods are Brazilian rather than African; second, they speak Portuguese rather than some obscure African dialect. The most popular of these local deities are the Old Black Slaves, or Pretos Velhos, and the Amerindians, or Caboclos.

In its early days, Umbanda was treated as a subversive movement, and the centres were frequently raided by the police. But today Rio radio broadcasts programmes devoted to Umbanda, and newspaper kiosks sell periodicals that deal openly and frankly with Umbanda matters. Through a friend of a friend, I made arrangements to visit an Umbanda centre and one Saturday afternoon introduced myself at a place called the Palácio de Oxalá, run by a certain Pai Fernando. This centre—a newish, three-storey building—was situated on the Ilha do Governador in a moderately prosperous middle-class suburb. Pai Fernando's house was attached to it. The forecourt was a curious place. Bits and pieces of the paraphernalia of Umbanda lay strewn around: effigies of the spirits, pots full of rotting chicken covered in a scab of flies, and cages of live chickens waiting to be ceremonially sacrificed. The sweet, sickly odour of decay pervaded the air.

Pai Fernando was not at home, but in the Palácio I met one of his Filhos de Santo—a neat, soft-spoken and friendly man dressed entirely in white, who in his working life was a bank manager in Rio. He would be happy to show me round the Palácio, he said, although I would not be allowed to enter certain rooms: on the previous evening, he explained, there had been an initiation ceremony and now some of the initiates were secluded in the rooms at the back of the centre and could not be disturbed.

To ward off evil spirits, a beach-goer includes on her necklace of charms a plastic figa— an amulet in the shape of a clenched hand, with the thumb protruding between the first and second fingers. Figas, seen everywhere in Rio, are considered to be effective only when they are received as gifts.

The Filho first took me into the Umbanda assembly room, which was more elaborate but less spacious than the Candomblé one I had visited. The altar was thick with religious effigies: Christ, St. George on a horse, St. Christopher dressed in skins and carrying a stave, and several versions of the Virgin Mary. We sat in a seat at the back and the Filho spoke about his own experience of Umbanda.

"I was dangerously ill," he told me, "and staring death in the face, so to speak. Medical doctors had not been able to help me and I was desperate. Then two lawyer friends of mine said I should try Umbanda, and they gave me Pai Fernando's name. My family were dead set against it and hired a private detective to see where I went and what I was up to, but I didn't care. I came to see the Pai and he talked to me and put his hand on me. And then I started to tremble all over and fell to the ground in a faint. The spirit of the saint had come to me, I suppose. After that I started to get better. It was extraordinary—I mean, look at me now, fit as a fiddle. So I became very interested in Umbanda, very convinced about it, a believer, and so did the private detective who had been following me. Then one day I decided that I wanted to be initiated, and the Pai said, 'Fine'. So that's what I did. I have no regrets. Umbanda saved me from death and now it fulfils my life. My family have come to accept it. And so has the bank where I work. In fact, a third of my staff are Umbandistas now."

While we were talking, we were joined by Pai Fernando, a most impressive person who radiated an aura of energy and moral strength. He was a big man, light-skinned and in his late forties. He combined an air of informal friendliness with an innate authority—a man, I should imagine, to whom those in need would readily turn for succour and solace, a sort of family doctor and local priest, psychiatrist and social worker rolled into one.

Besides running the Umbanda centre, which entailed four late nights each week, the Pai was also a full-time major in the Brazilian Air Force and worked in the engineering wing at the big air base on Ilha do Governador. In the 1950s he had been one of Brazil's leading pop singers, but turned his back on fame and riches in order to pursue his deep interest in Umbanda. I went back with him to his house and he played some of the records he had made. In one of them, *Cânticos de Umbanda*, he sang 11 Umbanda hymns to the accompaniment of a choir, drums, an electric organ and the sound effects of thunder, wind, waterfalls and machine-gun and artillery fire. Before I left, we arranged that I should attend the Umbanda session at 9.30 p.m. on the following Monday.

When I arrived on that Monday evening, the session began almost at once with the entry of the mediums, the Sons and Daughters of Saint. They took up their positions in two semi-circles—the men on the right of the altar, the women on the left. The women were attired in long white Bahian dresses, the men in white trousers and T-shirts. Then a little bell rang and drums started beating and the Mãe Pequenha (the Little Mother, next in order of authority below the Pai de Santo) brought in an incense burner to purify the room, swinging it about in much the same way that priests do in Catholic services. Next, she presented it in turn in front of all the mediums, who held out their hands in the smoke, spun around on their feet, and made the sign of the cross.

Afterwards all the mediums crouched down, and the Pai de Santo knelt before the altar and intoned a prayer, while the Mãe Pequenha sang a ritual hymn of purification in preparation for the second stage of the meeting, the summoning of the Orixás. The cleansing process was not complete, however, until the members of the congregation had been purified as well. This was done by the Mãe de Santo (next in order of authority after the Mãe Pequenha), a big, black woman wearing many beads around her neck, who smoked a cigar and knelt on a magic chalk mark—a star shape composed of many intersecting lines called a *ponto riscado*, or Orixá's symbol. She muttered and beat her head on the ground, while all the mediums uttered a strange hissing sound and made dusting motions around their heads, as if driving the evil spirits off like flies.

Then the mediums sat down on benches at one side of the room and the members of the congregation queued up to be successively purified by the Mãe. Each stood in front of her while she blew cigar smoke over them, made cleansing motions with her hands and pressed their hands between hers. In this way she expelled the unclean or malign elements, which were then received by the mediums on the benches, who all convulsed as if they had received an electric shock. After everyone had been purified, the drums and singing and dancing began again. Now I was about to see the mediums going into trances.

Every Orixá has his own drum-beat and song, and when he hears these, so the Umbandistas say, he comes down from his astral home and occupies the body of a dancer. The medium is commonly referred to as the "horse", and when the spirit comes down and possesses him, he is said to be "ridden". The medium then speaks and behaves with the characteristic voice and gestures of the spirit. Oxalá, for example, speaks in a trembling moan; Xangô will repeat the sound *ei-i-i*; Oxóssi howls like a dog; and Oxun goes *hum hum*.

As the drums beat, the dancing mediums one by one entered a state of trance. They would stagger suddenly as if they had been shot; they would groan, cry out, arch their backs, tear at their hair, tremble violently, roll their eyes, fall to the ground, laugh crazily and pull agonized, contorted faces. One young Filho hobbled around like an old man with one arm bent behind his back; apparently he had been seized by an Old Black Slave.

The congregation was not exempt from these trances. A white man in a business suit went into a prolonged fit, spinning wildly on his heels and shouting strange noises and firing an imaginary rifle. He had presumably been seized by Oxóssi, the god of hunting, and he had to be coaxed out of his seizure by one of the mediums, who blew cigar smoke over him. A respectable middle-aged white lady sitting in front of me went into a fit of hiccups and beat her hands about her head to drive off a swarm of invisible spirits. Altogether about 30 people in the room appeared to be affected by an extreme form of psychic change.

Then the music stopped and the people got down to the main purpose of the evening: the consultation with the spirits. Now that the Orixás were present, the congregation were at liberty to ask help from them through the voices of the mediums. Each in turn was purified again by the mediums, who passed a lighted candle across the supplicant's body in front and behind. Then the person wanting advice engaged—through the medium—in a private consultation with the saint; I had no way of discovering what was being discussed. A little before midnight, the session came to a quiet end with prayers and hymns. The congregation sat with their eyes shut and heads in hands. Finally the Pai and Mãe and all the Filhos and Filhas filed out as calmly as though they were choristers in an English village church.

I slipped away to collect my thoughts. It was well past midnight when I got back to Copacabana. There, fortified by a large steak in a crowded seaside restaurant, I contemplated the oddness of the scene I had just left. I had no doubt that, for many of the people involved, the trances were genuine—a form of self-hypnosis induced by the drumming, singing, and ritual incantation. But were the participants really "possessed" by the various Orixás and saints of the Umbanda pantheon? Surely not. Surely they only thought they were. And yet, what about inexperienced mediums who are seized by obscure and unfamiliar spirits they do not know about and visibly embark on a bad trip, much to the consternation of their fellow mediums? What of the mediums who, when in a trance, speak languages they do not know, and possess knowledge they could not possibly have? What about the miracles shown on television and attested by doctors?

I dipped my steak in the pepper sauce and stared out to sea, watching the faint trace of the white surf beating on the darkened beach. Having seen my fellow human beings so preoccupied with things that I could not perceive myself, and having heard all I had heard in Rio, I realized I must keep an open mind. I could not scoff.

Festival for Yemanjá

Amid ceremonial banners and pennants, spiritists gather round a statue of Oxalá, the supreme god of Umbanda, that has been set up on the Copacabana sands.

Every New Year's Eve, the wide beaches of Rio undergo an extraordinary one-night transformation, changing from pleasure grounds for devotees of sun and surf into sanctuaries for believers in Umbanda, the city's largest spiritist sect. As the sun sets, a great throng of the faithful congregates on the sands to commune with various deities of the cult and pay special homage to the ruling divinity of the sea, Yemanjá. Gathered beside bonfires and candles, they swirl to the mesmerizing beat of drums, consult mediums about their problems, and chant hymns: "Yemanjá, my mother, pity us and help us. For though the world is great, your strength is even greater." The climactic moment comes at the stroke of midnight, when the worshippers rush to the water's edge and address a final plea to Yemanjá for her favour during the year ahead.

In a rounded depression in the sand, lighted candles reveal magical signs that are probably of African origin.

Champagne, beer, and other offerings are laid out to lure Yemanjá, whose portrait appears in the foreground.

Summoning the Spirits

To tempt Umbanda gods into the mortal realm on Yemanjá's great night, the celebrants resort to rituals tailored to each deity's special characteristics. Mystical symbols, inscribed in the sand or picked out by votive candles, are a key part of the summoning ceremonies. But the spirits expect material tribute as well, and so the worshippers come prepared with food, drink and all manner of presents that will facilitate their quest for divine succour.

A spiritist kneels beside candles set in a cross. Umbanda incorporates much Catholic imagery, and Yemanjá herself is closely associated with the Virgin Mary.

Armed with a ritual cigar, an elderly Umbanda medium shuts her eyes and concentrates on the problem of a man who has sought her out for spiritual advice.

Surrounded by a shadowy army of onlookers, a group of worshippers treads an orderly course around a candlelit sand altar erected for the goddess of the sea.

In the grip of a trance, a medium whirls before the serene effigy of Yemanjá.

The Enchantment of the Drums

As Yemanjá's festival gathers momentum, worshippers engage in dances intended to draw spirits into their bodies. Some of the movements are carefully choreographed, but with the approach of midnight more and more participants are taken with wild seizures. They gyrate or writhe on the sand until the spirit finally releases its hold, leaving them exhausted.

A woman wades into the Atlantic rollers to surrender a bouquet to Yemanjá.

Offerings Bequeathed to the Waves

The instant the New Year is ushered in, the Umbanda faithful surge into the surf and cast forth a multitude of propitiatory gifts—flowers, mirrors, combs, jewellery and even sacrificed animals. If an offering is washed back on to the beach, Yemanjá has rebuffed the supplicant, but if it is carried out to sea, her future aid and protection are thought to be assured.

Rejected by the sea goddess, a solitary rose that represented a request for supernatural favour lies stranded on the shore by the morning's outgoing tide.

6

The Greatest Show on Earth

All through February, Rio had been getting hotter and hotter. On some days the temperature soared to more than 100°F and the blistering city canyons were as humid and steamy as the Amazon rain forest. As the thermometer rose, so did the nervous excitability of the Carioca, for every day that passed brought the city nearer to the disintegration of reality, the ritualized anarchy of the pre-Lenten bacchanalia known as Carnival. Drivers began to drive more wildly and accidents were more frequent now. One day I sat in the back of a taxi in a traffic jam in the Copacabana Tunnel, and the taxi-driver, in his nervous frustration, began to play a samba rhythm on his headlamp dip-switch. Soon all the other drivers were doing the same and the tunnel was full of flickering headlamps—music transformed into light, a silent, purely visual street band.

One Saturday before Carnival, I lunched with a friend at an open-air restaurant along the Avenida Atlântica. We sat at a round metal table in the shade of a large café umbrella, turning our faces to catch any puff of breeze that might blow in from the sea, and ordered *feijoada completa*—the splendid black bean, rice and meat set-piece of Carioca gastronomy—with a rum cocktail to start and a big bottle of cold beer to accompany the meal. It seems extraordinary, looking back, that in such scorching weather we should have had an appetite for such a heavy meal. But we ate and drank like cowhands after a cattle drive and we were in an expansive mood by the time we first heard the drum.

The drum! To be exact, a *surdo*—the big, deep bass drum of the samba band, a Hercules among instruments, the backbone and pillar of the samba, a metronome with a tick like Big Ben. The beat of the big drum exploded in our ears, impelled us to our feet, and drew us, beer in hand, towards the source of the sound, like moths to a candle.

The street band, one of many such amateur groups that tour the various districts of the city as Carnival draws near, was composed of men who were nearly all black and for the most part beyond middle age. After the initial fanfare of the *surdo*, other instruments—tambourines, kettle drums, trumpets, trombones and saxophones—joined in, filling the spaces between the main beat, the relentless *bom bam bom bam bom bam* of the big drum, with arabesques of sound. The music was urban, folk and baroque—old Carnival favourites that were gay and sad by turns, extroverted yet reflective, bitter and sweet. The brass-players' cheeks inflated and deflated like bellows as they forced their breath through their contorted instruments; the drummers bom-bommed and rat-tatted with deadpan faces;

At the climax of the Carnival festivities that consume all of Rio before Lent, members of one of the city's Samba Schools—huge neighbourhood clubs that train all year long for a single great parade—make their rhythmic way down Avenida Presidente Vargas, cheered on by 80,000 spectators in the stands.

the traffic slowed, the cafés emptied, the golden boys and girls drifted up from the beach, and everyone began to sing and dance on the pavement.

Drum hypnosis, they call it in Rio. For the samba is like the plague: it stalks the streets and enters people's homes. You cannot resist it, you can only flee or succumb. As my inhibition evaporated, my feet began to move in time with the music, my knees bobbed, my hips wobbled, my shoulders swayed, my arms involuntarily shot out, and on my lips I was surprised to hear strange words of Carnival incantation.

"*Oba! Oba!*" I exclaimed, looking shiftily about me. And then, more boldly, I sang: "*Obaba-Ola-o-Baba!*"

People all about me were singing these words, which came from a captivating new samba song called *No Reino da Mãe do Ouro*, "In the Realm of the Mother of Gold". This salvo of samba on the seafront of Copacabana gave me my first whiff of Carnival gunpowder, my first warning of the barrage to come.

Carnival is not exclusive to Rio, nor even to Brazil. It is regularly celebrated in various other cities in the Catholic regions of Europe and the Americas, a ritual last fling before Lent. The word itself is derived from the Latin phrase *carnem levare*—to give up meat—which in popular usage was corrupted to *carne vale*, or meat farewell. In some cities this pre-Lenten jollification goes under other names. In Munich, for example, it is called Fasching; in Nice and New Orleans it is known as Mardi Gras, which is the French name for Shrove Tuesday. But nowhere else in the world is Carnival celebrated as riotously and as sumptuously as it is in Rio de Janeiro. There, it is total Carnival.

The festivities always start on the Saturday before Ash Wednesday and last for four days and four nights—a public holiday reserved for sleepless merry-making during which the wheels of government and commerce grind to a halt. Because Carnival in Rio is a deliberate descent into chaos, the four-day period can be extremely confusing for outsiders. In the resulting hurly-burly, it is difficult to separate the various elements that make up the whole, and it would be foolish to try—the whole point, after all, is to feel rather than think. But if I was to have a clear picture of Carnival, I realized, I would have to establish the groundplan in my mind during the final countdown. So as the preparations proceeded all over Rio, I went to rehearsals, talked to people who would play some of the leading parts in the revels, and began to unravel the mysteries of the most disorderly and spectacular festival in the world.

Basically, I found, Carnival is celebrated in two ways. On the one hand, there is an indoor Carnival of public balls and private parties—the Carnival of the middle and upper classes. On the other, there is an outdoor Carnival of street parades—the Carnival of the lower classes, but with an increasing middle-class participation. The outdoor Carnival can be sub-divided into

A task-force of seamstresses, working towards the moment when their Samba School will compete in the Carnival parade, assembles costumes in the club headquarters. The shelves in the background hold an array of trophies won by the school in past years.

the small, informal street parades of friends and neighbours, and the great public parades, or *desfiles*, of highly organized, competitive dance groups. The most notable of these groups are the giant Escolas de Samba or Samba Schools, which for more than 20 years have provided the single most important spectacle in Rio's Carnival: the big *desfile* that takes place in the city centre and lasts from Sunday evening through to Monday afternoon. It is this parade that most visitors think of when they hear the word Carnival.

Like so much else in Rio, modern Carnival is the result of long inter-mingling of European and African traditions. The early Portuguese colonists had brought with them a crude form of pre-Lenten revelry called the Entrudo, during which noisy battles were fought in the streets and people carried out mock invasions of their friends' houses, squirting one another with water or throwing flour, soot, eggs and anything else that came to hand. The Entrudo carried on in this form for nearly three centuries. In the meantime, the African slaves in Brazil developed their own kind of Carnival festivity, based on the rhythmic percussion and tribal dancing of their old homelands.

In 1853 the Entrudo was banned because it was considered too primitive to be celebrated by the people of a civilized metropolis. It was gradually replaced by a less rowdy, more expressive kind of celebration. Battles were still fought, but with streamers and confetti, not water and flour, and many other kinds of revelries took place simultaneously. Informal groups called Blocos—consisting mainly of servants, slaves, labourers and other poor people—roamed the streets in a haphazard fashion, beating drums, frying pans, tin cans and anything else that came to hand. Other groups called Ranchos, mostly made up of Portuguese immigrants, paraded through the city with small bands and pageants based on religious motifs. Wealthy organizations bearing the name Great Societies, financed and run by businessmen and men of letters, put on much more elaborate pageants in the city centre, with large floats and hired revellers in fancy dress accompanied by big brass bands. And in the theatres, clubs and big houses, grand balls were held, thronged by masqueraders in the classical costumes of pantomime—Harlequin and Columbine, Pierrot, and Scaramouche.

By the beginning of the 20th Century the various festive forms of modern Carnival had been worked out, but the music had not. Anything and everything was played, from old-fashioned European waltzes, polkas and schottisches to more genuinely Brazilian music—the light and graceful *choros* of small guitar and woodwind street orchestras, the slow doleful marches of the Ranchos, and the naughty *maxixe* dance music of the downtown bars. All that changed in the century's second decade. A new generation demanded a new kind of Carnival music—and got the samba.

The samba took shape when a group of young Carioca musicians began to combine traditional African rhythms with Portuguese folk songs popular at the time. The rhythm of the samba, with its deceptive 2/4 beat, its counterpoint of half-beats and rests and cross-currents of artfully stitched and syncopated percussion, is contagious in itself. When it is accompanied by the samba dance, which derives from an Angolan dance whose movements simulate the act of copulation, it becomes thoroughly irresistible. The samba gained prominence in 1917 when a tune called *Pelo Telefone*, "On the Telephone", became a Carnival hit and was the first samba to be made into a gramophone record.

All over Rio during Carnival, neighbourhood Blocos began to adopt this new kind of music. The Blocos of the favelas and poorer areas of the city went one step further: they also borrowed the parade style of the Ranchos. But unlike the Ranchos, which took complete bands with them, the favela Blocos took only a percussion band—the *bateria*. Some of them called themselves Samba Schools.

The first Samba School was founded in August, 1928, in the district of Estácio by a small group of like-minded samba musicians—*bambas do samba*, they were called, or masters of samba—who used to meet regularly in the Bar Apolo on the corner of Pereira Franco Street. Individualistic and often religious men, they wrote lyrics like poets even though they were often illiterate, and they composed melodies of great beauty even though they could not read a note. Their Samba School first appeared in public at the Carnival of 1929, parading in good order among the brawling Blocos and the rowdies and rogues who seethed in the Praça Onze de Junho, a down-at-heel square in the rough quarter of town. Although the school was soon disbanded, its success led to the formation of others. By 1933 there were 25 competing Samba Schools parading in and around

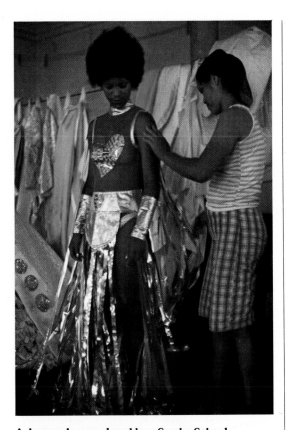

A dressmaker employed by a Samba School makes final adjustments to the glittering regalia of a sambista—a dancer who will take part in the school's forthcoming Carnival presentation. Club funds pay the cost of attiring the main dance corps, but every school has enthusiastic members who provide their own costumes and join the big Carnival parade.

the Praça Onze de Junho, which remained their spiritual home until it was largely redeveloped in the 1940s. Each school wore different colours— green and rose, for example, or blue and white—and provided a focus for the underprivileged and hungry people of its own favela or district, who supported it with massive partisanship.

Today, the Samba Schools are great institutions with bureaucratic structures and officers elected at annual general meetings. In the best schools, the composers, dancers and musicians are occupied with Carnival every day of the year. As soon as one Carnival is over, they begin preparations for the next. The purpose of each Samba School's pageant in the big parade is to unfold an *enredo*, or theme—to tell a story through the combined media of dance, music and visual display. By May, a Samba School will have decided on the theme of its pageant; by August, the composers will have worked out various sambas based on the theme; and by October, the best samba will have been chosen. Meanwhile, the artists and support staff will have created the *fantasias*—the luxurious and fantastical costumes to be worn by all the performers of the school—and the immense, ingeniously designed floats known as *alegorias*. By the beginning of November, the Samba School will be mobilized for rehearsals. Finally, all will be ready. *"É a hora!"* comes the rallying cry—"the hour has come!"

During the week before Carnival, Rio was buzzing with activity. In the Avenida Presidente Vargas and Avenida Rio Branco, where the main parades would take place, workmen were busy putting the finishing touches to grandstands and big, gaudy, overhead decorations. The Samba Schools and other Carnival groups—Blocos, Ranchos and Great Societies —were making frantic efforts to get the components of their pageants ready for a show that would be watched by millions. In their shacks in the favelas, charladies and washerwomen, street-cleaners and shoeshine boys tried out the opulent costumes that would transform them into the aristocrats of fantasy. More and more street bands appeared in Copacabana; they were there each night now, standing under the street lamps, blasting their cheerful music above the roar of the commuter traffic.

Some nights I went out to the rehearsals of the Samba Schools. Because of my prior acquaintance with the favela of Mangueira, I got to know its Samba School and some of its participants better than any of the others. The Mangueira Samba School had some outstanding members. Most notable of all was Waldemiro Teixeira, who had been head of the *bateria* since 1935 and had won more Carnival awards than any other *bateria* director in Brazil. He was a shaky old man with a big, blobby, pitted nose and a few teeth leaning like old tombstones in his gums, and he lived alone in a hut at the top of the hill that had been his home since 1914. He had never married, he told me, but he had a son—at least, he believed it was his son—who lived down in the town. For 25 years he had worked as a labourer loading stones on to lorries to be carried away for the building of pavements in Rio, and it was only in his spare time that he had trained the *bateria*. But in 1967 one of the lorries backed into him and injured him so badly that he lost his job. He was given a small pension by the Samba School and was able to devote all his time to Carnival.

The decibel level of a *bateria* at full blast is immense. Waldemiro used three different whistles to direct the performance. The best, he said, was a plastic one made in England and called the Acme Thunderer. It had three different pitches—one to start the *bateria*, one to stop it, and one to call for special dance turns by the standard bearer, the *porta-bandeira*. Waldemiro's two other whistles were also made in England. One, the Rocket International Fifty-One, had a lovely, calming sound and was used to signal a moderate dancing pace. The other, gold in colour, emitted a high, piercing shriek; it was ideal, he said, for accelerating the *bateria*— and, for that matter, everything else.

He blew on the gold whistle to demonstrate its effect. The band went into quick-time. Drumsticks twirled like camshafts, hands flickered over blurred tambourines, the dancers gyrated until they dripped with perspiration. A peep or two from the Rocket International settled the Samba School back into a more measured tempo.

Most of the members of the Mangueira Samba School, as in other Samba Schools, were humble working people—lift attendants, labourers, maids, lorry drivers' mates. Many of them had to save up one and a half months' pay, going without meat for months on end, to defray the cost of the elaborate Carnival costumes. Their expenditure in time and energy was no less great. For example, one drum player in the *bateria* was a road sweeper who did not get home to the favela until 7 p.m. But at 10.30, after a supper of thick pea soup with onions, he descended the hill to the *quadra*, and spent several hours in gruelling rehearsal.

Mangueira's samba for the forthcoming *desfile* was the song I had already heard, the one with the refrain *Obaba-Ola-o-Baba*. It was the smash hit of Rio before Carnival began. I was to hear it night and day until Ash Wednesday, the end of Carnival—and then the song, apparently unsinkable, vanished as completely as the Titanic. The composers of this enchanting number were Herlich Fonseca (known as Tolito) and Rubens da Mangueira—natty and self-composed gentlemen who had prospered from their work. When I met Tolito, he was wearing a white felt hat, bright pink shirt and tight white shoes—the typical dress kit of a *bamba*. "A samba," he told me, "is born naturally, all at once in the head. You don't compose it; it comes." After he had worked out the notation of a song with the help of his son's saxophone, he asked his friends to sing it to see how they liked it. If they didn't like it, he threw it away. "People seem to like *Obaba-Ola-o-Baba*," I told him. Tolito shrugged and turned away, his mind ringing up royalties like a till.

At an informal evening rehearsal in one of the favelas, a samba dancer swirls to the rhythm of an agogô—two linked steel cones that are beaten with a rod.

On the afternoon of Saturday, Carnival in Rio was declared open by the Carnival king, whose duty is to go the rounds of clubs and localities all over Rio, commanding the festivities to begin. Into the streets poured Carnival groups of all sorts and sizes. More than 80 Blocos, accompanied by large bands, began a big parade in the city centre. Small bands struck up their music in the side streets, gathering around them groups of revellers who disported themselves in a variety of disguises.

Any disguise seemed to go—the more bizarre the better. I saw an adult wheeled about in a pram like a baby; a child wearing the grotesque rubber mask of a very old man; good Christians dressed up as Satan; blacks painted as whites, and whites painted as blacks; the poor in the fine clothes of the rich, the rich in the guise of beggars; the living disguised as the dead (the skeleton motif was very popular); and men dressed as women, with huge painted lips, two-inch false eyelashes, immense protuberant breasts and high-piled hair-dos of grotesque coloration. One minced across the square towing a yellow toy poodle on wheels: "*Chuchu!*" he shrieked. "*Vem cá!* Baby! Come Here!" Carnival lovers with big black beards and bright red bras planted smacking pantomime kisses on each other's rouged, clown-like cheeks. Along the pavement dashed a sultan pursued by a hairy slave girl. "I'm coming to get you," barked the slave girl, "I'm coming to get you." And in the gutter, a portly, middle-aged man waltzed by with the stuffed dummy of a gorgeous-looking girl attached to him by an elastic band round his waist.

As the outdoor Carnival gathered momentum, similar astonishing scenes presented themselves at every turn. The sound of drums and tambourines, trumpets and euphoniums echoed through the streets of Rio, and poorer Cariocas all over the city succumbed to a collective hysteria heightened by beer and the hypnotic effect of the samba. At the same time, away from the sight of the street revellers, even more riotous scenes were taking place. At night, lavish masquerade balls were held at dozens of private clubs and one or two of the big hotels. Most of these balls were exclusively for the rich. An entrance ticket for two could set you back nearly $85; a table might cost as much as $350, and a box for 10 more than $1,700. If you wanted champagne, you had to pay nearly $170 a bottle, and whisky cost $10 a glass.

During the course of Carnival I attended several of the big balls, and by the end I had learned to dance on tabletops like everyone else. But it was my first ball, the *Havaí*, or Hawaii, as it was known, at the Rio Yacht Club, that made the greatest impression. Situated at the edge of Botafogo Bay beneath the granite ramparts of Sugar Loaf, the Rio de Janeiro Yacht Club is one of the most expensive and exclusive clubs in Rio. You can join by paying $22,000—with no obligation to own a yacht or take to the water. Generally the Yacht Club is a model of propriety and discretion, but on the night I went there the atmosphere became licentious in the extreme.

A workman carefully applies red paint to the lips of a plaster Eve that will ride on the deck of a Samba School float, or alegoria. Floats express some facet of an overall Carnival theme chosen by the Samba School, and their narrative ingenuity is one of the factors in the selection of a parade winner.

The ball each year is based on a South Pacific theme, but it resembled nothing so much as a Roman orgy. Imagine the scene: A tropic night so hot and sultry that only a fool would wear more than next to nothing. In a large space open to the starry sky and delimited, it seems, only by the darkness beyond the coloured festival lights, fountains play round a brilliantly lit coral-green swimming pool. Several samba bands on rostrums blast Carnival music above the uproar of several thousand revellers. Most of the women are almost naked. They are, in the main, white women deeply bronzed from days spent stretched out on the South Zone beaches. They have removed every follicle of body hair and wear *tangas* whose token particles of cloth are tailored to a biological nicety. *Quanto menos melhor*—the less the better—is their motto. They are, by and large, in ecstasy. So that they can be better displayed, they stand on the tables among the warm champagne and ice cream melting in hollowed-out pineapples, and they vibrate to the samba in gestures that neatly demonstrate the sinuousness of their mobile parts. Every so often a hairy male will extend an index finger in the direction of a female abdomen and prod the lady's belly button. She, with undulatory motions, will revolve around the finger like the man (so the joke goes) who plays gramophone records by running round them holding a gramophone needle.

I had never seen anything like this before. Men and women samba-ed into the pool and disappeared, still swaying. Girls sat on their boyfriends' shoulders like horsewomen riding stallions and were carried around the dance floors. I had to fight my way through the crowd, buffeted by thighs, crushed by bottoms, and occasionally even lifted right off the ground by the sheer press of flesh.

In this massive assertion of femalehood at the society balls, it is not difficult to see an act of social and sexual revenge and liberation. The middle- or upper-class Carioca woman, although more emancipated than most women in Brazil, has not achieved the sexual equality of some of her European and North American counterparts. She is still confined to a kind of Latin-American family purdah, while the head of the household, whose word is still law, is free to seek amorous adventures elsewhere. In baring her body to the gaze of other men, in moving it to a dance whose motions closely resemble the act of love, the Rio woman evens the score in one ritualized act of promiscuity.

Not that her behaviour is always purely symbolic. Carnival is an opportunity to achieve romantic ambitions, a time when Cariocas can turn their fantasies into reality. There is a special expression for this yearly phenomenon: *namorado de Carnaval,* or Carnival affair. Under the smoke screen of Carnival hysteria, normally respectable husbands can run off with young girls, and young bachelors can elope for an hour with normally faithful wives. But fantasy and reality coexist uneasily in Carnival when it comes to affairs of the heart. The murder rate increases sharply, and many of the deaths are results of *crimes passionels*—acts intended to solve the eternal triangle by the simple process of knocking off one of the corners.

Such Carnival excesses seem profoundly puzzling to many outsiders, and even Cariocas are hard-pressed to find explanations for their pre-Lenten behaviour. What is it that causes the city to erupt in this way? Why does a bourgeois housewife stand on a table and display herself in front of thousands of people? Why does a respectable businessman dress up as a clown and turn cartwheels up and down the street? Why do so many of the city's poor reduce themselves almost to beggary in order to dance through the streets in fancy dress?

I began to understand Carnival myself only when I realized that it is a deliberate reversal of all norms. Everyday distinctions between worker and boss, rich and poor, black and white are forgotten. For four days the Cariocas can shed the burden of their usual personalities and become whomever they please. Those to whom no one normally listens are given a hearing; those who are alienated can find brotherhood in the mayhem of the streets. Familiar rules, familiar values are interred and replaced by fresh ones in a symbolic triumph of the forces of life over the forces of death. In such ways, men and women can release the pent-up neuroses and strait-jacketed emotions of daily existence and liberate primal drives that normally lie deeply hidden.

A good example of the escape from social norms is provided by the homosexual celebrations that take place in Rio during Carnival. For a few days, gay men can be their own true selves. They come not only from Rio but from other parts of Brazil and from overseas as well, and they have their own transvestite ball—the so-called *Baile das Bonecas*, or Dolls' Ball, one of the most remarkable of the grand Carnival events. Some 3,000 people attend the Dolls' Ball in downtown Rio, and their appearance is extraordinary. With the help of silicone injections, hormones, make-up, extravagant costumes and assumed names—Suzie Wong, Verushka, Anouk—the Dolls create a world of illusion they wish could be reality. They vamp and coo in a weirdly ersatz atmosphere of theatrical high camp. But they behave with discretion. Above all, this ball is for show.

During my rounds of Carnival revelries, I stumbled on another gay get-together that was very different. It was an obscure function, not advertised and far from the tourist beat. It was not to my taste, but I was advised that there I would hear the best Carnival music played by the best Carnival band in the best Carnival ambience in the whole of Rio. So, a little after midnight I set out for the venue, a ramshackle dive called, optimistically, the Elite Club, situated on the first floor of a turn-of-the-century house in a dimly lit street in a decayed area near the docks—an underworld district of tarts, crooks, rats and alley cats.

It was dark, hot, crowded and noisy inside the Elite. Several hundred men and a few women were crowded into a space about the size of a large

Costumed processions with music and dancing became part of Rio's Carnival during the slave era. In this lithograph, based on an 1830 water-colour by the German artist Johann Rugendas, black Cariocas perform in a noisy pageant called the Congada, commemorating the kings and queens of their Congo homeland.

drawing-room. At one end there was a rough, wooden bar, and at the other a dais with drummers, trumpeters and trombonists playing on it. Neon strip lights covered in blue and pink paper cast a wan light on the gathering, and ceiling fans stirred the fetid air. An illuminated little shrine of the Virgin Mary look down incongruously at the dancers, surveying the whole dis-armingly frank and intimate scene. Most of the dancers were stripped to the waist, partly because of the heat. Most were young. The band played loudly and marvellously, and as the crowd moved to the rhythm of the samba, the floor bounced up and down. It flexed so violently that I became frightened and retreated to the comparative safety of the wall. At the club's previous premises, I was told, the floor had given way and all the guests had fallen through into the basement below—but the band had never stopped playing.

A balcony ran round three sides of the room, looking down on the dance floor. Hoping to escape the heat and the crush, I climbed up to it. There I discovered an American friend of mine sitting at a wobbly table in front of a tape recorder almost buried beneath empty beer bottles. He was a student of pop music and urban folk-cultures: hence his presence at the Elite and the tape recorder.

"Douglas, my friend," he shouted above the din. "It took me four years to find this sink of iniquity and you have found it in one night. This is the authentic scene, my friend. This is the raunchy armpit of Carnival."

invasion of Northern Europe on D-Day. As the hot hours passed, they rehearsed their steps, tuned their drums, adjusted their perukes, checked their floats and practised their songs. From this amazing assembly, an overpowering uproar rose to the heavens.

The 41 Samba Schools were divided by merit into three groups, and they had to parade down two separate avenues. Groups 2 and 3 were to go down Avenida Rio Branco, and Group 1, containing the top 14 schools, down Avenida Presidente Vargas. It was this latter group that most people wanted to see. The main *desfile* course was 750 yards long and was lined with grandstands for 80,000 or more spectators. Each school had 75 minutes to cover the distance, and during this time they would unfold their chosen *enredo*, or pageant theme.

A Samba School's presentation follows the same basic form each year. It is divided into sections, or frames, separated from one another either by an *alegoria*, or float, or by a walking "curtain" of dancers. Within each frame a part of the theme is developed by a mixture of components— visual or aural, human or inanimate—each with its own point to make. By government decree, all themes must focus on some aspect of Brazilian history or culture. Thus, in the parade I watched, one Samba School chose as their theme the Negro art of Bahia; another chose the Portuguese navigators' first discovery of Brazil; another dealt with the gods of Candomblé; and another with a pre-Columbian civilization revealed by archaeological findings on the island of Marajó in the mouth of the Amazon. Out of such heavyweight materials the Samba Schools managed to manufacture a confection as light and scintillating as vaudeville or a Hollywood spectacular.

Near the end of the *desfile* course, a team of judges would mark each school's performance on both the quality of its parts and the coherence and impact of the whole. The contest is fought as keenly as a football championship, not only because there are tens of thousands of cruzeiros in prize money at stake, but also because the Samba School that received the lowest marks in Group 1 would be replaced by the top school of Group 2 the following year.

The Group 1 *desfile* always starts later than the advertised time of 6 p.m. I reached the grandstands in the Avenida Presidente Vargas well after 8 o'clock and the procession had only just begun. In the adjacent streets, *sambistas* milled around in their fancy costumes—the *fantasias* on which they had spent so much time and money—waiting their turn on the parade course. Next to the hot dog stalls, bewigged black men and women in 18th-Century French attire danced around squeezing mustard and ketchup on to their frankfurters. Everywhere there was the rattle of tambourines and the beat of drums. The excitement was infectious, and not at all inhibited by the hordes of policemen standing about with sullen looks. They perhaps had reason to be rankled: a crowd of the poorer Carnival-goers, unable to pay for a seat in the stands, had climbed on to

Four Carnival revellers transform their everyday selves with masks made of materials ranging from silver paint to dyed feathers. The masquerading impulse of Carnival achieves its most spectacular expression by night, at grand costume balls attended by the rich.

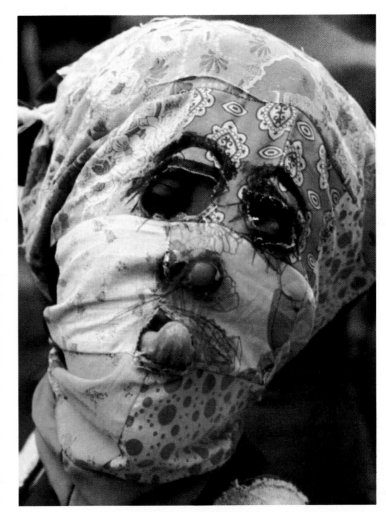

the vehicles in the car park so that they could peer over the barricades. As a result, the roofs and bonnets of the cars were hopelessly dented.

My Press pass allowed me to go anywhere I wished on the parade course. Here, the atmosphere was bewitching. The avenue, brightly illuminated by coloured lanterns and overhead television lights, was like a long funnel of light in dark, empty space. It seemed as though the real Rio and the real world had mysteriously vanished and this half-mile of fantasy and illusion was the only reality that existed.

The *desfile* itself was mesmerizing. Samba Schools passed down the course like passenger liners steaming through the Suez Canal. The first section of each Samba School was the *abre-ala*, or opening wing; it consisted of a group of *sambistas* with or without a float, bearing the name of the school and their *enredo*. Then came the *comissão de frente*, or front committee—10 to 15 venerable *sambistas*, usually in top hats and tails, who were the directors of the school. The main body of the *sambistas* followed them. These came in various forms. According to Carnival regulations, at least one of a school's groups of dancers should be composed of women in traditional Bahian costumes. In addition, each Samba School had a *mestre-sala* (master of ceremonies) and *porta-bandeira* (standard-bearer), who danced as a couple and formed one of the key elements of the presentation. There were also *passistas* and *pastoras*, male and female dance specialists who performed spontaneous, non-choreographed samba dances; *ritmistas*, who played musical instruments while dancing; *destaques*, isolated and sumptuously decked-out figures who stood motionless on floats or walked among the dancers, and represented principal characters in the story; a *puxador do samba*, who sang the lyrics of the *enredo* non-stop for more than an hour, usually on a trailer bearing a small guitar group and amplifying equipment; and, of course, the big percussion band, the *bateria*.

As each Samba School passed down the course, I was stirred most of all by the *bateria*. It was the heart of the pageant; without its beat the whole spectacle would have perished. From far off you could detect the approach of each *bateria* by the thudding of the *surdo*, the huge bass drum laying down the beat like a great piston, one beat every second—*boom bam boom bimbim boom bam boom bimbim*. So explosive was the sound that you could feel it through your feet, transmitted along the surface of the concrete avenue. Within the intervals formed by this big mesh of sound, there was a complex weave of smaller sounds. Other drums played intermediate beats, forming meshes for the still-smaller sounds of the tambourines, rattles, frying pans, *reco-recos* (notched rods grated with a stick), *agogôs* (steel cones beaten with a rod) and *cuícas* (friction drums). The only sounds not in unison with this complex, perfectly woven tapestry were the piercing whistles of the *bateria* directors, who were like ships' captains passing orders down to the engine-room.

A solo dancer in a Carnival pageant accompanies his steps with a smile.

A female dancer glides along under a formidable weight of costumery.

Silver leaves cascade from the spectacular costume of a destaque, an isolated figure who represents a character in the story told by the Samba School's pageant.

I can think of nothing in the world quite like the Rio Carnival parade. The Moscow May Day parade is comparable in size and popularity, but not in purpose or spirit—and all other carnivals are pint-sized by comparison. The samba and the scale—these are the keys to the pre-eminence of the Rio Carnival. The costumes, taken individually, border on kitsch, and you can see the same sort of finery and the same sort of floats at the London Palladium or the Lord Mayor's Show. But send them out into the street in such prodigal numbers as this and infuse them with the life-giving pulse of the samba, and the effect is overwhelming. When a *bateria* goes by, the crowd stands up—all 80,000 onlookers—and samba in the stands with their arms stretched out, like sun-worshippers, towards the source of the music. Even the hard-bitten newspaper and TV reporters and the stern judges in their boxes are infected. They samba with the rest.

I found the *desfile* not only impressive but strangely moving. It affected me in much the same way that the equivocal revelries at the Elite Club had done. As the night wore on and the schools passed by, I became uneasily aware that, for all the joy I saw around me—the gyrations of the *ritmistas*, the syncopations of the *bateria*, the sexy charms of the half-clad *pastoras*, the gutsy formation-dancing of the stout Bahian matrons, the sinuous dignity of the *mestre-sala* and *porta-bandeira*, the warmth and enthusiasm of the crowd—what I felt was not so much joy as sadness. Why did I feel sad? Was it me? Was it indigestion, a surfeit of black beans? Was it a pang of recognition of the immutability of the human condition— an awareness of the desert that lay beyond this mirage, the bare lives to which these temporary princes and princesses would soon return?

Or was it because, being physically so close to them and sometimes among them, I saw the agony behind the gaiety? To sing and dance in costume, non-stop for 75 minutes, down a half-mile stretch of concrete, between a canyon of grandstands that cut off the breeze on a hot and tropical night, is an immense feat of physical endurance. The temperature that night was 92°F. Behind the fixed grin and the bouncy samba step I could see the sweat and gritted teeth. As the night passed and the next day broke and the sun rose higher and higher, the *desfile* became not celebration but flagellation, like running a gauntlet. By the time each school had reached the judges' box at the far end of the course, some *sambistas* were in a state of collapse.

I saw one person twitching with heat stroke on the ground, unable to rise as her dance group moved remorselessly on. I saw several other *sambistas*, their plumes and finery trailing in the dust, carried away by ambulancemen against the current of the parade. I saw a *destaque*, a man, lifted in a state of semi-coma off his float, where his only task had been to remain motionless in the stifling heat. Throughout all this, the grim men of the *baterias* beat their instruments as relentlessly as sadists, giving no quarter to the thousands who panted in their wake. The percussionists, too, suffered, but they would not give up; the palms of their hands were blistered and torn and there was blood on their drumskins, but they were the iron men of Carnival—they would play to the end of time.

The advent of daylight dispersed the curiously enchanted atmosphere of the *desfile*, but not its irresistible vitality. The television lights looked green now, casting a pale ocean-bottom glow on the Carnival flotsam of beer cans, streamers and trodden-on samba song sheets. The crowd, after 12 hours in the stands watching nine of the schools go by, were not appreciably diminished in numbers or enthusiasm. They were more tired, more drunk, and less well-clad than they had been, and in the intervals between Samba Schools they leaned against each other and fell asleep. But all in all, their stamina was as remarkable as that of the participants.

And so the gay-sad, sane-mad, real-unreal pageant of black, brown and white men, women and children passed by: a *comissão de frente* in silver top hats and tails; a big *alegoria* of polystyrene dolphins, sea-horses and whales that resembled huge piranhas with teeth; a plastic hand the size of a lorry with a life-size dummy *mãe pequenha* sitting in it; a "mermaid" with a long silver tail that she moved from side to side; a group of Queen Nefertitis; a *bateria* of sultans and rajahs; 50 sun gods in Inca king headdresses.

The *sambistas* of the Mangueira favela, whose leading members I had met during rehearsals, were almost the last to set off down the scorching half-mile of the *desfile* course. By now the sun was high in the sky and there was no breeze. The *sambistas* must have been exhausted before they even started; but when they passed the judges' box they were still performing as if Carnival had only just begun, and the crowd, too, were still shouting for more. On the approach of the *bateria* directed by Waldemiro Teixeira, thousands of voices joined in the chorus of Mangueira's hit samba: "*Obaba-Ola-o-Baba* . . . It's the mother of gold who's coming to save us. . . ." This mass rendition was punctuated by Waldemiro's whistles, the Acme Thunderer and the Rocket International Fifty-One, as he directed his juggernaut *bateria*, driving them all on, on to the end of the *desfile*, on to glory.

It was after 2 o'clock in the afternoon before the last of the 14 Samba Schools of Group 1 passed the judges' box and crossed the finishing line. At that spot, a spreading, smelling overflow from the overburdened public urinals marked their transition back from the unreal to the real world. Sealed off by a cordon of mounted police in steel helmets, they disappeared into the jams of the Monday afternoon traffic in the direction of the shanty towns from which most of them had come.

Monday evening, Tuesday and Tuesday evening came and went. The round of Carnival balls and private parties continued, the Ranchos paraded to their traditional marches and the street bands continued to blast their music. And so Ash Wednesday approached. At the last of the Carnival balls, everyone sang *Cidade Maravilhosa*, one of the evergreen Carnival songs, for the last time. Then we all drifted home.

The party was over. Still dressed as a Bedouin from the sands of Arabia—my disguise at the last ball—I walked home through the streets of an exhausted city, dragging my feet among the old paper streamers and the scattered remains of huge paper flowers that littered the pavements like jetsam washed up from some immense shipwreck. A grey pre-dawn light began to illuminate the streets, revealing sepulchral shapes in door-ways and gutters, human figures in every posture of somnolence, as still and slumped as in death. They were mostly young, these worn-out revellers of the night, and mostly poor. Many lay clasped in each other's arms—pierrots and pirates huddled against mermaids and princesses. A few people stirred as I shuffled past and looked up with sightless eyes. I caused no surprise in my outlandish garb, for they saw me as one of their own kind. Relieved of the stricture of my own identity, I had become—by empathy at least—one of them.

"*Bom Carnaval*," murmured a Satan with horns and a fork tail lying in a shopfront at the end of the Copacabana Tunnel. I opened my mouth to reply, but found I had lost my voice. In the bedlam of the ball, I had sung and shouted too much.

In the east, a deep red sliver of sun rose above the craggy silhouette of the Morro de Leme. The sky lightened rapidly. Along the edge of the surf on Copacabana Beach a man dressed as Neptune and brandishing a trident pursued a girl in a *tanga* and fairy wings; he soon overtook her and, locked together, they subsided into the frothy white spume of the surf; in the cooling waters of the Atlantic Ocean the lovers thus assuaged their Carnival heat. The sun continued to rise and in a few moments had cleared the point. One after another, the lights in the windows of the apartment blocks went out, extinguishing the human shadows that flickered intriguingly on walls and ceilings.

Men and women who had slept on the beach rose singly and in pairs, brushed the sand off themselves, stared at the sun and the sea, and shuffled away. A fat black man who lay curled beside a silver drum he had beaten to bits looked ruefully at the remains of the drum skin and carried the instrument away in his arms like a dead baby. One by one the fantasy people of the night, the figures of masque and allegory and disguise, left the stage. In their place came noisy busloads of schoolboys from the North Zone, out for the day at the seaside. Elderly early-risers, freshly shaved and pomaded after a good night's sleep, paddled contentedly at the edge of the sea and collected sodden Carnival hats and wooden cutlasses washed up by the tide during the night.

I turned away from the sun and the real world and sought a few moments of sleep in my room. The sound of the surf was soon drowned by the sound of the traffic, but I did not wake.

The morning papers carried the Carnival post-mortem. According to the statistics provided by the Instituto Médico-Legal, 125 people had ended up

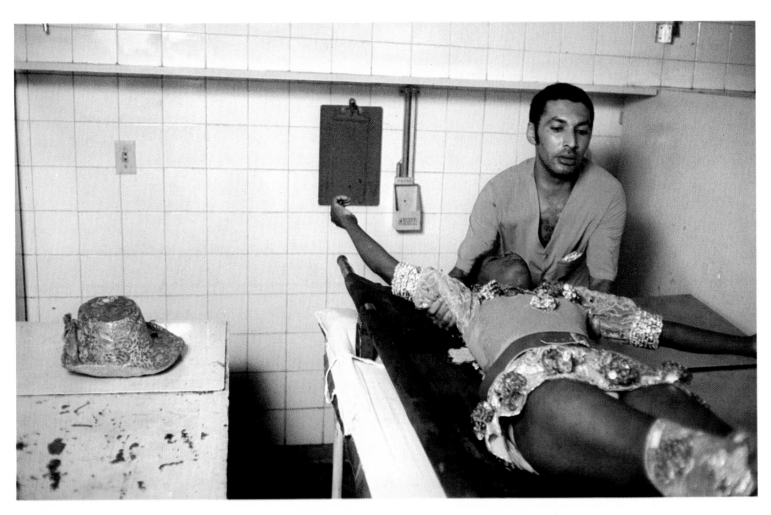

Felled by heat exhaustion during one of the parades, a sambista is gently lifted from a stretcher by a hospital attendant. Hundreds of people require treatment for heat stroke as the festivities run their course, and one year 50 were crushed to death in the crowds.

in the mortuary in the city of Rio. Many of them had been crushed to death in the crowds, but the toll also included 17 people who had been murdered, 6 drowned, 1 asphyxiated in sand on a suburban beach and 35 killed in road accidents. There had been 1,271 arrests, and 16,136 hospital casualties, including nearly 1,000 cases of alcohol poisoning. In general, the police agreed, it had been a more peaceable Carnival than some.

As for the *desfile* of the Samba Schools, opinion was divided. According to the critics, the Samba School from the district of Portela had done a lovely pageant with a rotten samba. Mangueira had had too many floats, but the *bateria* was terrific. Beija-Flor had been visually the prettiest of all the schools, and their samba was well sung.

On Friday, the official results of the *desfile* were announced. The Beija-Flor Samba School, which came not from the city of Rio but from Nilópolis in Greater Rio, was declared the winner. Mangueira came a close second. The judges seemed to admire Beija-Flor's visual display more than its music. This, said some critics, indicated an unwelcome shift away from samba and animation towards luxury and lifeless set-pieces. The *desfile* was no longer a competition between *sambistas*, they complained, but between architects and engineers and scenic designers.

There is an evident truth in this. From being part of popular urban folklore, the Samba Schools are becoming part of the show-business industry. The total cost of putting on the big *desfiles* is now the equivalent of two or three big-budget movies. In order to stay in the top rank, the Samba Schools have had to rely more and more on the services of professional set designers, costumiers and musicians, all paid at top rates. Gradually, middle-class white members are attaining more important positions in the schools, and because of the high cost of tickets, only the middle and upper classes can afford to watch the *desfile* from the grand-stands. So the poor, whose celebration this is, have become extras in a commercial spectacular, and the major event of Carnival is being cut off from its roots.

Who knows what will happen to Carnival? Already the informal cele-brations of the traditional street Carnival are in decline, hit by urban re-development and by the all-consuming gigantism of the big parades. Perhaps Carnival will go the way of professional football. Already it has clubs, leagues, competitions, cups and prizes, colours, expenses, stars, fans, a TV audience and big business interests. Will there one day be Carnival Pools and a Carnival World Cup? Will a time come when Mangueira will take on the Mardi Gras flower pelters from Nice, when Beija-Flor will slug it out against the London Lord Mayor's Show, and Portela, after beating the Moscow May Day marchers, will go down 3-1 to the beer swillers from the Munich Bierfest?

The morning after the announcement of the *desfile* results, I went back to the Mangueira favela to see what the Samba School people thought of this year's Carnival and how they were faring in defeat. It was atrociously hot, over 100°F and very humid. I discovered the founding fathers—the elders of the tribe, so to speak—in a little barber's shop on the main street.

I entered and sat down. Beer came and we talked, brushing away the flies and the sweat. A baby was crying at the back and an open drain gave off an evil smell. A tall, thin, elderly black man was sitting in the rusty old barber's chair, which had stuffing coming out of the cushioning. He was Peri Fragoso, a well-known composer of samba. He sat back meditatively, his eyes shut and his hands clasped over his stomach, while the barber scraped away at his chin with a cut-throat razor. Three other old black men sat in the room or leaned in the doorway. One of them was Waldemiro, who had just won two prizes in the Carnival—one from a Rio television station, TV Globo, and one from the Mayor—for long service as the best *bateria* director in Carnival.

"This year was best of all," said Waldemiro. "We got 15 points out of 15 for the *bateria*. But it was hard. We didn't enjoy it. It was like a war. The avenue was a hot tunnel without ventilation. If a man fell down, another man took his place. Just like a war."

Another black man confided: "True Carnival is not there. It is here in the favela. Down there in parade we don't do it for the fun. We do it for the glory." The others concurred. All those people who paid to come and cheer—it was the glory.

The composer in the barber's chair sat bolt upright with the lather round his ears and addressed the room loudly. "We are poor!" he declared, "But we are free!" And then he sat back, eyes tightly shut again.

More cold beer was passed through the tatty door curtain. Outside in the blistering heat a bread seller strode up the favela street, blowing bugle calls on an old army trumpet to attract the customers. On the other side of the street, a young black man in an advanced state of drunkenness was dismantling a wooden-frame Carnival beer stall by the simple process of attacking it with a hammer. He lurched at it with flailing arms, rained blows, on it, and under the momentum of his inebriated assault fell on it and toppled to the ground as the wreckage crashed about his ears. Time and again he repeated his attack, while a crowd gathered to jeer and cheer. Every time he fell he was picked up, given back his hammer and let loose on the infuriating beer stall again.

Observing the stall wrecker crawling slowly on his hands and knees after yet another attack, a man in the barber's shop, a former president of the Samba School, remarked: "The human being is 70 per cent alcohol and 30 per cent salt. When it becomes 80 per cent alcohol, it grows weak."

"Were you upset about the results?" I asked.

"No, no," one of the men replied. "No, no. Beija-Flor were worthy winners. We did all we could, but it was the will of God that we took second place to them. It is just that we *should* have won! The judges gave us the wrong marks for our *fantasias*."

"But we did win!" cried another. "Beija-Flor are not from Rio city. So we were the best of all the Samba Schools of Rio."

"Yes!" yelled the man in the barber's chair sitting up again. "The Press and all the other bigots didn't like us, but we stuck in their throats!" He fell back in his seat, silent again.

The ex-president produced Waldemiro's trophy from TV Globo—a statuette of a *ritmista* on top of a pedestal that was inset with a picture of the late Natalino José de Nascimento (known as Natal), one of the earliest and most revered of all Rio's *bambas do samba*. He held the trophy close to him—communing, he said, with Natal's spirit—and there were tears in his eyes. He handed it to Waldemiro, whose hands shook as if with fever.

"I have won lots of trophies," said Waldemiro. "I have been in every one of Mangueira's Carnivals. I have taught generations of children to play in the *bateria*. But I have never made a cruzeiro out of it. For 22 years I was a stonemason's labourer. But when I had my accident the company never paid me any compensation or anything. Now I have got nothing. I used to drink, but I can't do that now. Sometimes I wonder if it was all worth it."

"Of course it was," said the ex-president, staring out at the slum that had been his home for three decades of his life. "What would you have been without Carnival? What would any of us have been?"

Samba Mania

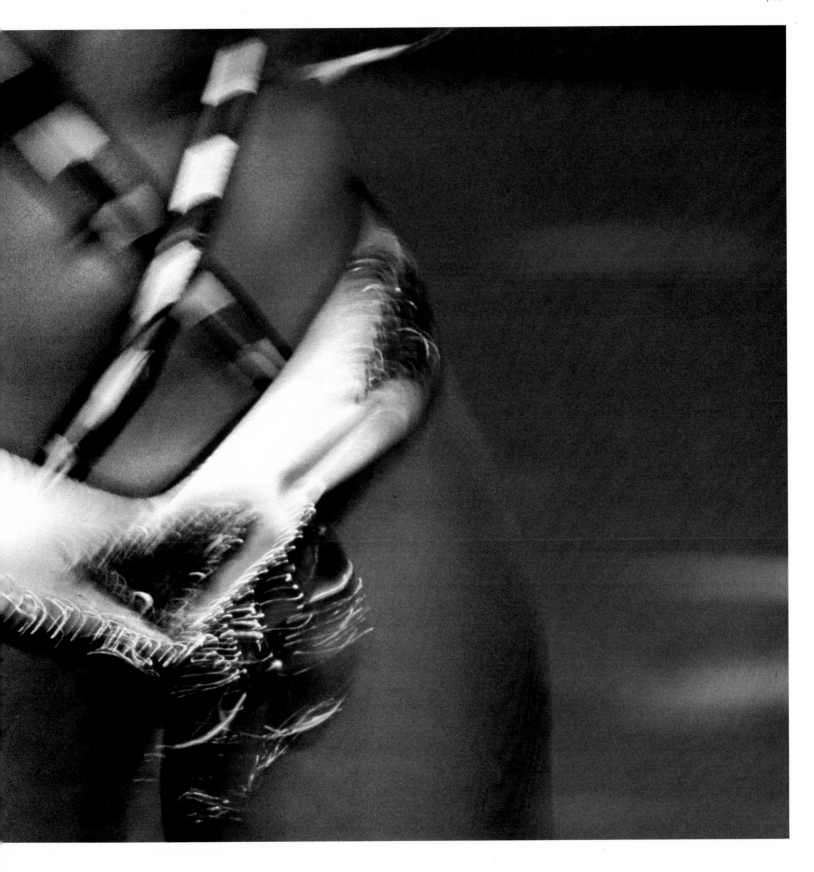

During Carnival, Rio abandons itself unashamedly to the samba. Crowds of dancers throng the city's ballrooms, streets and squares, and the whole metropolis seems to dissolve into a blur of motion paced by the pounding rhythms of tambourines, rattles and batteries of drums. Sometimes the samba is fast, thrusting, and—especially when performed by girls in bikinis —consciously erotic. In the official parades, the dance is a set piece of decorous choreography. At all-night balls, it becomes an exercise in alcohol-inspired improvisation. And when practised by groups from the hill slums, it is an excuse for milling about in the streets and playing the fool. Whatever form it takes, the samba is danced to the verge of human endurance. As Ash Wednesday dawns, 96 hours of dancing mania take their toll and the city succumbs to exhaustion.

Bibliography

Balsamo, José, *O Amor em Alta Rotividade* in *O Caso Lou* by Carlos Heitor Cony (ed.). Civilização Brasileira, Rio de Janeiro, 1975.

Bandeira, Manuel, and De Andrade, Carlos Drummond, *Rio de Janeiro em Prosa e Verso.* José Olympio, Rio de Janeiro, 1965.

Bishop, Elizabeth, *Brazil.* Life World Library, New York, 1963.

Boxer, C. R., *The Golden Age of Brazil.* Cambridge University Press, London, 1962.

Brooks, John (ed.), *The 1977 South American Handbook.* Trade and Travel Publications, Bath, 1976.

Bryans, Robin, *Fanfare for Brazil.* Faber and Faber, London, 1962.

Burns, E. Bradford, *A History of Brazil.* Columbia University Press, New York and London, 1970.

Cabral, Sérgio, *As Escolas de Samba: o quê, quem, como, quando e por quê.* Fontana, Rio de Janeiro, 1974.

Centro de Conservação de Natureza, *A Floresta de Tijuca.* Rio de Janeiro, 1966.

Costa, Lúcio, *Arquitetura Brasileira.* Ministério da Educação e Saúde, Rio de Janeiro, 1952. *Plano Piloto para a Urbanização da Baixada compreendida entre a Barra da Tijuca, O Pontal de Sernambetiba e Jacarepaguá.* Prefeitura do Rio, Rio de Janeiro, 1976.

Cruls, Gastão, *Aparência do Rio de Janeiro (2 vols.).* José Olympio, Rio de Janeiro, 1965.

Da Costa, Edmundo Luiz, *Rio in the time of the Viceroys.* J. R. de Oliveira & Co., Rio de Janeiro, 1936.

Da Costa, Lamartine P., *Capoeira sem Mestre.* Tecnoprint, Rio de Janeiro, 1975.

De Alencar, Edigar, *O Carnaval Carioca através da Música.* Freitas Bastos, Rio de Janeiro, 1965.

De Azevedo, Fernando, *Brazilian Culture.* Macmillan, New York, 1950.

De Barros Latif, Miran, *A Comédia Carioca.* Rio de Janeiro, 1962. *Cidade No Trópico—São Sebastião do Rio de Janeiro.* AGIR, Rio de Janeiro, 1965.

Debret, J. B., *Viagem Pitoresca e Histórica do Brasil.* Livrario Martin, São Paulo, 1940.

De Castro Maya, Raymundo Ottoni, *A Floresta da Tijuca.* Editores Bloch, Rio de Janeiro, 1967.

De Holanda, Sérgio Buarque (ed.), *Historia do Brasil.* Difusão européia do livro, São Paulo, 1967.

Delano, Anthony, *Slip-up.* André Deutsch, London, 1977.

Ender, Thomas, *O Velho Rio de Janeiro, através das gravuras de Thomas Ender.* Edições Melhoramentos, Rio de Janeiro, 1958.

Evenson, Norma, *Two Brazilian Capitals.* Yale University Press, New Haven and London, 1973.

Ferrez, Gilberto, *A Muito Leal e Heróica Cidade de São Sebastião do Rio de Janeiro—Quatro Séculos de Expansão e Evolução.* Banca Boavista, Rio de Janeiro, 1965.

Fodor's *1977 Guide to South America.* Hodder and Stoughton, London, 1977.

Freyre, Gilberto, *The Masters and the Slaves.* Weidenfeld and Nicholson, London, 1956. *The Mansions and the Shanties.* Weidenfeld and Nicholson, London, 1963.

Gardel, Luis D., *Escolas de Samba.* Kosmos, Rio de Janeiro, 1967.

Gibson, Hugh, *Rio.* Doubleday, Doran and Co. Inc., New York, 1937.

Goldwasser, Maria Júlia, *O Palácio do Samba: Estudo Antropológico da Escola de Samba Estação Primeira de Mangueira.* Zahar Editores, Rio de Janeiro, 1975.

Goodwin, Philip L., *Brazil Builds: Architecture New and Old 1652-1942.* Museum of Modern Art, New York, 1943.

Henderson, Keith, *Palm Groves and Humming Birds.* Ernest Benn, London, 1924.

Joffroy, Pierre, *Brazil.* Studio Vista, London, 1965.

Kellemen, Peter, *Brasil para Principiantes.* Civilização Brasileira, Rio de Janeiro, 1963.

Kubitschek, Juscelino, *Por que Construi Brasilia.* Editores Bloch, Rio de Janeiro, 1976.

L'Architecture d'Aujourd'hui: *Brézil,* numbers 42-43, Paris, 1952.

Mackenzie, Colin, *Ronald Biggs—The Most Wanted Man.* Hart Davis, MacGibbon, London, 1975.

Maurois, André, *Rio de Janeiro.* Collection Merveilles de la France et du Monde, Paris, 1951.

Marshall, Andrew, *Brazil.* Thames & Hudson, London, 1966.

McGregor, Pedro, *The Moon and Two Mountains.* Souvenir Press, London, 1966.

Michelin, *Green Guide to Brazil.* Paris, 1976.

Ministério da Educação e Cultura, *Cultura, No. 19,* Brasilia, 1975.

Perlman, Janice, E., *The Myth of Marginality: Urban Poverty and Politics in Rio de Janeiro.* University of California Press, Berkeley. London, 1976.

Poppino, Rollie E., *Brazil, the Land and the People.* Oxford University Press, New York and London, 1968.

Quatro Rodas, *Guia do Rio,* Editora Abril, São Paulo, 1977.

Rebêlo, Marques (ed.), *Guanabara. Brasil, Terra e Alma.* Marques Rebêlo, Rio de Janeiro, 1967.

Rugendas, João Maurice, *Viagem Pitoresca através do Brasil.* Martins, São Paulo, 1949.

St. Clair, David, *Drum and Candle.* Macdonald & Co., London, 1971.

Silva, Fernando Nascimento (ed.), *Rio de Janeiro em seus Quatrocentos Anos—Formação e Desenvolvimento da Cidade.* Distribuidora Record, Rio de Janeiro, 1965.

Skidmore, Thomas, *Black into White—Race and Nationality in Brazilian Thought.* Oxford University Press, New York, 1974.

Smith, T. Lynn, *Brazil—People and Institutions.* Lousiana State University Press, Baton Rouge, 1963.

Stern Magazine, *Rio—Die schönste Stadt der Welt verkommt.* Hero Buss, photographs by Robert Lebeck, Hamburg, January 5, 1977.

Studio Huberti, *Artistic Guide to Rio de Janeiro,* Rio de Janeiro, 1922.

Velho, Yvonne Maggie Alves, *Guerra de Orixá: um estudo de ritual e conflito.* Biblioteca de Antropología Social, Rio de Janeiro, 1975.

Wagley, Charles, *An Introduction to Brazil.* Columbia University Press, New York, 1973.

Wellington, R. A., *The Brazilians.* David and Charles, Newton Abbot, 1974.

Zweig, Stefan, *Brazil: land of the future.* Cassell and Co. Ltd., London, 1942.

Newspapers and periodicals:
Brazil Herald, Rio de Janeiro; *O Cruzeiro,* Rio de Janeiro; *O Dia,* Rio de Janeiro; *Gente,* Rio de Janeiro; *O Globo,* Rio de Janeiro; *Jornal do Brasil,* Rio de Janeiro; *Manchete,* Rio de Janeiro; *O Pasquim,* Rio de Janeiro; *Time Magazine,* New York; *Veja,* São Paulo; *Visão,* São Paulo.

Picture Credits and Acknowledgements

Sources for pictures in this book are shown below, with the exception of those already credited. Credits for pictures from left to right are separated by commas; from top to bottom they are separated by dashes.

All photographs are by Art Kane except: Cover—Luis Villota. Front end paper—Alair Gomes. Page 10, 11—Loren McIntyre. 14, 15—Map by Hunting Surveys Ltd., London. Silhouettes by Norman Bancroft-Hunt. 16, 19—Loren McIntyre. 20—Robert Ostrowski. 36—Loren McIntyre. 40—Luis Villota. 43—Loren McIntyre. 47, 48—Loren McIntyre. 52, 53—Loren McIntyre. 54, 55—Leo Hetzel. 70—Loren McIntyre. 73—Biblioteca Nacional, Rio de Janeiro. 74—Piedade Rato, Ajuda Library, Lisbon. 76, 77 —Manchete, Rio de Janeiro. 88 to 97—British Library Board. 98—Claus Meyer, Black Star. 103—Leo Hetzel. 105—Luis Villota. 106—Loren McIntyre. 107—Douglas Botting. 108, 109 —(top, pic. 2) Loren McIntyre—(middle, pic. 2) Loren McIntyre —(bottom, pic. 3) Leo Hetzel. 113—Robert Ostrowski. 114, 115 —Loren McIntyre. 117—Claus Meyer, Black Star. 132—Claus Meyer, Black Star. 134, 135—Loren McIntyre. 136—Leo Hetzel. 140—Romano Cagnoni—Loren McIntyre, Loren

McIntyre. 141—Leo Hetzel. 142—Vieira Queiroz. 143—Claus Meyer, Black Star. 146—Loren McIntyre. 152, 153—Loren McIntyre. 154, 155—Romano Cagnoni. 156 to 161—Loren McIntyre. 162—Bruno Barbey from Magnum Photos. 167— Alair Gomes. 171—Alair Gomes. 173—Bibliothèque Nationale, Paris. 177—(top) Bruno Barbey from Magnum Photos, Alair Gomes. 179—Douglas Botting. 183—Romano Cagnoni. 196, 197—Bruno Barbey from Magnum Photos.

The author and editors wish to thank the following: Acadêmia de Capoeira, Rio; Glória Anderson, Rio; Suelly de Barros Latif, Petrópolis; Regina Berardo, Rio; Leslie Bethell, London; Ronald Biggs, Rio; Rosa Maria Bortoni, Rio; Anna and Katy Botting, London; João Pimental Brandão, Rio; Marcelle Soares Brandão, Rio; Brazilian Embassy, London; Brazilian Navy, Rio; Brazilian Tourist Office, London; David Briggs, Rio; Roberto Burle Marx, Rio; Canning House Library, London; Sra. Carmalita, Rio; Bruce Corrie, Petrópolis; Pai Fernando Costa, Rio; Lúcio Costa, Rio; Major Luis Alberto Cutrim, Rio; Charles Dettmer, Thames Ditton, Surrey; Milton Drucker, Rio; Wim van Dyke, Petrópolis; José Gallo, Rio; Susan Goldblatt, London;

Albert Goldman, New York; Alair Gomes, Rio; Liz Goodman, London; Ewa Grabowski, Rio; George Hawrylyshyn, Guaratiba, Rio; John Hemming, London; Phuong Nga Hillenbrand, Rio; Beatriz Horta, Rio; Dick and Roberta Huber, Rio; Hélio Jaguaribe, Rio; Jamelão, Niterói; James Jauncey, London; the late President Juscelino Kubitschek; Elizabeth Loving, London; Greville and Margaret Mee, Rio; Frances Middlestorb, London; Jean Miller, Texas; Antonio Olinto, London; John Stanley Pickston, Rio; Dr. Ivo Pitanguy, Rio; Príncipe Dom Pedro de Orléans e Bragança, Princesa Dona Cristina de Orléans e Bragança and Princesa Dona Maria Joana de Orléans e Bragança, Petrópolis; Margaret Quick, London; Maria Teresa Rende, Rio; Brigadeiro João Camarão Telles Ribeiro, Rio; Augusto Rodrigues, Rio; Jayme Garcia dos Santos, Rio; Bob Saunders, England; Anthony Smith, London; Peace Sterling, Rio; Sr. and Sra. Hans Stern, Rio; Dr. Marcos Tamoyo, Rio; Waldemiro Teixeira and the Mangueira Samba School, Rio; Deborah Thompson, London; Stephanie Thompson, London; Cynthia Vance, Rio; Sra. Arminda Villa-Lobos, Rio; David Villiers, England; Zico, Tonito and the members of the Flamengo Football Team, Rio.

Copyrights

Index

Numerals in italics indicate a photograph or drawing of the subject mentioned.

Colour reproduction by Irwin Photography Ltd., at their Leeds PDI Scanner Studio.
Filmsetting by C. E. Dawkins (Typesetters) Ltd., London, SE1 1UN.
Printed and bound in Italy by Arnoldo Mondadori, Verona.